TOYOTISM, Root of Lean

a new paradigm of work and management that dominates the changing times, beyond COVID19

Contents

Prologue _ Toyotism, the wisdom of 'Insight' obtained through 'Sight'

Intro _ Toyotism, the principle of survival of the fittest, more urgent in times of crisis

PART 1. Toyotism, a different perspective on work

Chapter 1. Japan's failure, Toyota's success

American-style management vs. Toyota-style management

Toyotism, which recognizes people as a source of profit

The fall of other Japanese companies that failed to turn knowledge into work

Chapter 2. Paradigm change and understanding of world affairs

What is a paradigm?

From labor to task, from task to work

Chapter 3. Toyotism, a new insight into work

All industries are the creation and transcription process of ideal information.

The difference between Fordism and Toyotism in terms of looking at work

An era where the creation of ideal information becomes money

A new perspective on work, from the input to the output

Chapter 4. Creative Labor and Enterprise Labor, Understanding Values and Added Values

Maximization of value work and value-added work in the Toyota method

Toyota first recognized the superiority of information originating from customers

Chapter 5. Understanding Control and Management

The survival inequality of a company through value

Both sides of work, must be changed while maintaining

Toyotism is a continuation of maintenance and improvement

Chapter 6. Toyota's Philosophy That Reveals Problems

Problems in the existing PDCA cycle

Toyota starting from C for visualization

Toyota focuses on problem solving with abnormal response management

PART 2. Toyotism, the way of working is different

Chapter 7. Toyotism-based ways of working are Agile and Lean

Paradigm change according to the change of collaboration method

Toyotism represented by Agile and Lean

Chapter 8. Toyotism, working systematically

System is an organism

What does it mean to work systematically?

Four elements to build a system

Start of Toyota-style system work, automation

The four elements of the system and automation

Chapter 9. Visualization determines the success or failure of a system

A lot of things can be solved just by revealing a problem

It is a management problem, not a person, so a system is needed.

Chapter 10. Apple and Google imitate Toyota's cross-functional organization

The Obeya method that brought Toyota back up

Toyota's innovative team play, Shusa system

Toyota's way of working, project-type work focused on

horizontal linkage

Toyota's horizontal linkage system benchmarked by US companies

Chapter 11. Fostering human resources while solving problems

Toyota method focusing on problem solving

A culture that grows into talent through problem solving and reflection

Problem solving and human resource development through The three actuals, 3REALS

Chapter 12. Toyota's A3 Culture for Maximum Efficiency

A3 report as a work improvement technique for problem solving

8 steps of A3 thinking method and A3 report writing method

Chapter 13. Don't take countermeasures after death, but prevent them

Front loading and vertical start-up to solve the problem from the front

Prevention technique GD³ in the development stage

DRBFM, a creative prevention technique

Chapter 14. Toyota's New Values, TNGA

TNGA, a new platform to run Toyotaism

Toyotism is not a reverse idea, but common sense of our time

PART 3. Toyotism, work itself changes

Chapter 15. The Revolution of the Timely Production System (JIT)

Toyota's JIT production method outpaced the US automobile industry

The emergence of Lean companies benchmarking the Toyota method

Chapter 16. Tesla and Toyota, Partners for the Car of the Future

Google's Ivanpa Solar Power Plant vs. Tesla's Supercharger Station

Lean Company, Tesla, who practices JIT

Chapter 17. New Paradigm Partners, Google and Toyota

Social change led by Google's self-driving car

Google and Toyota lead the transition to a smart social system

Chapter 18. Toyotism in Germany, Industry 4.0

The goal of Industry 4.0 is Toyotaism

Industry 4.0 is a trend, not a paradigm

Chapter 19. The challenges of a new era found by successful companies in the 21st century

The new task of corporate survival according to the changing times

Outro _ Dreaming of Resourcism, another name for Toyotism

References

Prologue

Toyotism, the wisdom of 'Insight' obtained through 'Sight'

25 years in the consulting industry.

I've been working in this industry since 1996, so it's been 25 years since 2020, and from 2021, I'm moving towards a new 25 years.

Having spent 25 years as a consultant, I thought about what the mission of people working in the management consulting industry would be.

First of all, I did my best to serve as a consultant to spread methodologies for solving various problems. In particular, he has been in charge of benchmarking for excellent overseas companies for 25 years, and has endeavored to play the same role as a "industrial messenger" in the

Korean business history.

For 25 years, from Korea Management Association and Korea Management Association Consultants to today's Global Business Consulting, VE (Value Engineering) in the cost innovation field, IE (Industrial Engineering) in the production innovation field, TPM (Total Productive Maintenance), TPS (Toyota Production System), Six Sigma in the field of management innovation, and the ISO series of the International Organization for Standardization have been working to introduce and disseminate advanced methodologies and management innovation cases of excellent overseas companies to companies. What was my role in the knowledge industry as a management consultant?

In short, it seems to be 'generalization of special cases'. The methodologies that have led change in the industry were not imported to us only in the form of theory. As it should be said, success experiences filtered in the form of "innovative cases of advanced companies" in the US, Europe, and Japan were introduced along with the theory, minimizing the learning costs that companies have to pay. Many management consultants, including myself, have been working on "generalizing" the advanced methodologies that have been introduced in this way, rather than being 'special' and 'exceptions' that can be applied only to specific companies or organizations, but easily solved so that all companies and organizations can enjoy them.

Also, unlike a teacher or professor, the consultant job must produce results in the field. Because of these professional characteristics and circumstances, many colleagues working in the consulting industry must disseminate advanced theories and, on the one hand, verify and practice theories through trial and error applying them to companies in the field. By doing so, isn't my mission as a consultant to be a "preacher" who goes through the process of "generalizing" a "special" and fulfilling the role of a "practitioner" together?

Insight in sight.

In my Global Business Consulting, the essence of benchmarking is expressed in one sentence above. It means that you get 'Insight' through 'Sight'.

If readers can get a little "insight" of the essence of sustainable management through this book, I will be able to remember the last 25 years as rewarding from the starting point of the new 25 years.

February 24, 2010.

This is the day when Toyota Motor Company's president Akio stood and testified at a US hearing to deal with a massive recall that occurred in the US. Toyota Motor Corp. Set the shameful day as the "restart day," and made every effort to return to the basics and make a thorough re-leap. The reason for setting that day as an anniversary was not to reflect on the past, but to take it as an opportunity to take a new step toward the future. In addition, it was to prevent its meaning from weathering over the years.

On February 24, 2015, five years later, Toyota Motor Corp. finally started mass production of the hydrogen-fueled car "Mirai". Five years ago, President Akio's testimony at a hearing in the United States was wiped out, and he declared a "future" that will grow steadily with customers. They again showed that Toyota was at the beginning of the management pursuit. On February 24, the day of the re-start.

2016 marks the 80th anniversary of the establishment of Toyota Motor Corporation. Founded in 1937, it has reached exactly 80 years.

Toyota Motor Company, which produced 4,013 cars per year in only one factory in 1937, was the world's first in automobile production (11.13 million units), the world's first operating profit (2,750.5 billion yen), and market capitalization in 2014. It proved to be the best automobile company in the world by achieving 3 crowns in the first place (automobile sector, 22 trillion yen). As of 2020, it is the second largest automobile company in market capitalization after Tesla.

In retrospect, starting with Samsung Electronics' Toyota benchmarking in 2003, many companies in Korea flocked to Japan to benchmark Toyota, which could be called the Toyota Learning Frenzy. At that time, I was not in Korea. I have lived almost in Japan to serve as a way to convey the Toyota Way to employees in Korean companies. Those years lasted for years. And a turning point occurred. It was the Toyota Motor Recall. The Toyota recall at the time was a good example of the result of what we call growth. I think the Volkswagen diesel vehicle fuel economy situation clearly shows where the end of such 'expansion' intention is.

Why is it that people always describe the situation of increasing sales and increasing profits as "growth", and always say that "bubble" bursts when a situation of sharp decline is reached? I was always curious about this. Wouldn't that really reveal that the growth that many people enthusiastic about was actually expansion, not growth? Still, I wonder if we are still immersed in the collective unconscious of trying to ignore the difference between "growth" and "expansion".

If growth is to be transformed into expansion as it crosses a certain critical point, and the end of it ends with an explosion of expansion, which always bursts with bubbles, the recent performance of Toyota Motor Company and its remarkable rebound as seen earlier deserves a message. It is rather a lesson. Toyota's failure in the past few years when it tried to expand rather than grow. And on the bitter reflection that such an attempt is wrong, the solid success of the newly pursued growth shows that when and what actions can it be achieved?

This is my inevitability to publish this book at this point in time. This book is not intended to resonate with fans of the belated excuses and rediscovery of the Toyota method, which has rapidly cooled down since the Toyota Motor Vehicle recall in 2009. Through their reflection and achievement, I would like to talk about a deeper spirit, 'Toyotism as a paradigm', not a "way" that we can easily imitate and throw away. I deeply felt the importance of an essential understanding of the Toyotism-based way of working. Of course, just as Ford Motors and Fordism, which provided the industrial paradigm of the 20th century, have long since changed their tracks, Toyota Motors and Toyotism, which provided the paradigm of the 21st century industry, will someday change that path.

While working in the field, I have always emphasized the need to separate Toyotism from Toyota. In other words, what we need to see is not Toyota's remarkable performance or the success of a new leap forward. Rather, it is 'Toyotism as a definition of a contemporary task and a method of solving the task' that will contribute to the aspect of what our contemporary tasks are and how to solve them.

After distressing between human courtesy and consideration for readers, I decided to add greetings to those who still need to express gratitude at the end.

Since 1996, it has been able to benchmark more than 440 companies around the world and interact with more than 1,300 global talents. I feel thankful.

First of all, I am grateful to the advisors, including Mr. Kawai and Mr. Matsuura, who formed and led the GBC Advisory Group in cooperation with the launch of Global Business Consulting (GBC) in 2007. I am also grateful to Mr. Kokubo, former director of the Denso Technical

Training Center, Mr. Kankoji, a specialist in industrial relations at Toyota, and Mr. Takagi from Fujitsu.

Despite various difficulties while still in office, Chairman Shoji Kondo of Hino Motors, managing director Yamatani of Sawafuji Electric, President Yokota and President Ohara of Nets Toyota Nangoku, and President Nakagawa of Toyota Motor Company's design headquarters, in China. Makiuchi, president of Toyota Synthetic China subsidiary, Kamei, president of Yamasei China subsidiary, President Terazono of Isan Industries, China subsidiary, and President Naganuma of RAMPF, which supports Toyota Group in Europe, and manager Yoshida of Hino Motors in Shanghai, Toyota. I would like to express my gratitude to Sugino, Managing Director of TG Logistics, who informed us about the group's distribution and logistics. I would like to express my gratitude to Miyata President of Fujitsu Systems, General Manager Ishizuka of Fujitsu, CEO Kojima of Ryobi Group, and many other people who have interacted with the above-mentioned bosses and interacted with me for the activities of Lean Company other than Toyota Group.

And I would like to express my gratitude to my parents who gave birth and nurtured me and my origin for enabling interaction with all of these people. I would like to express my gratitude to my family members who endured and hugged me, who were always absent, to colleagues, seniors, juniors, and bosses who showed love and understanding through my school days and work life.

I feel anew that in order for a person to exist, so many people and the whole universe must devote their efforts. Nevertheless, I feel the limit that my gratitude cannot reach so many people and the whole universe. So now, here, I want to express my special thanks to all the people I can actually meet with.

Finally, I'm just grateful to the readers.

Summer 2020 Harry Lim

Intro

Toyotism, the principle of survival of the fittest, more urgent in times of crisis

In order to understand 'Toyotism', which I intend to focus on in this book, an understanding of 'Fordism' must precede.

In 1903, Henry Ford founded a car company named after him in Dearborn, Michigan, USA. That's the famous "Ford Motor Company." Ford Motor Company's greatest achievement is that it has opened an era of popularization of automobiles. Ford Motor Company made mass production of automobiles possible through a divisional assembly line using a conveyor belt in 1923. This method of production was named "Fordism" by Antonio Gramsci, an Italian intellectual and thinker. Today, Fordism symbolizes the accumulation system of mass production and mass consumption as "push production by plan".

'Fordism', which means 'Ford Motors' definition of work and the way it works,' is from an article titled 'Americanism & Fordism' in Antonio Gramsci's book Selections from the Prison Notebooks of Antonio Gramsci: Notes on Politics, published in 1934. It was first named 'Fordism'. At that moment, Ford was no longer a "special case" for a company, but was able to qualify for "generalization" as a 100-year-old way of working. The last 100 years refer to the 'era of mass production and mass consumption'. Ford's method has been a paradigm and toolbox that can be applied to anyone in solving the problem of mass production, a problem of the times when supply is always scarce than demand.

As the 20th century passes and the 21st century passes, the world faces a huge turning point. The most prosperous era of human history, an era of overflowing objects and information, has arrived. There is no longer a shortage of objects and information. The market, full of goods and information, has reached the stage of encouraging "destructive consumption," which induces consumers to buy impulse because it is no longer "because of old and broken" but "just new". The apparel industry is a leading leader in 'destructive consumption'. Now no one throws away clothes because they are worn out or punctured. The market is asking us to buy new clothes just because they are 'out of fashion'.

We must first understand deeply that this situation, that is, the situation of the times surrounding us has changed. Unlike the 20th century, the biggest difference and characteristic of the 21st century is that "materials and information" are not lacking, but overflowing. It is important to understand that the essence of all the changes around us that occur without hesitation in all directions of the so-called industry lies in the 'flood of goods and information', which is advocated as a 'free economy'.

When the situation of the times changes, of course the tasks of the times also change. Now, it has become a world where Fordism's logic no longer works. This is not the era of 'selling what's made', but the era of 'making what's sold'. It is "Toyotism" to be referred to in this book that plays the role of a paradigm and tool box to respond most effectively to these contemporary challenges.

In the era of mass production, Fordism led the development of mankind in the last century with the slogans of "simplification," "standardization," and "division of labor," and the symbol of "conveyor belt". Simplification, standardization, and division of labor enabled us to achieve our goals by setting rules and sticking to them. At that time, the word management meant 'control.' Maintaining rather than changing is the source of competitiveness.

On the other hand, Toyotaism is the slogan that only companies that solve all three corporate management tasks: 'autonomation (quality)', JIT (just in time, delivery), pursuit of full work, and cost)' can be chosen by customers. It is leading the development of humanity in the 21st century holding the symbol of the demolition of the conveyor belt. Now, it is argued that simply repeating yesterday's work today cannot meet the heights of customers who are upgrading, and that way, they cannot survive by receiving the customer's "choice". At this time, the word management means 'change'. In other words, changing, transforming, is the source of competitiveness.

The fierce competition for survival in the ecosystem is "natural choice," said Charles Darwin. To explain that only those who have adapted to change survive, Darwin is said to have used the term 'natural choice' as a counterpart to 'artificial choice'.

In this book, I wonder whether the fierce competition for survival in the so-called industry and in our human world should be called "artificial choice". However, market selection is different from natural selection. Whatever happens in the industry, whatever it is, seldom happens naturally. Winners and losers are separated in the conflict between products and services obtained as a result of the active understanding and efforts of stakeholders.

In that sense, this book may be a book that actively denies Darwin's natural selection. Because in this book, I aim not to simply explain the present of the surviving things (natural selection), but to explain the future by actively dealing with what kind of thoughts and actions to survive in the market (artificial selection).

We will not look at Toyota Motor Company in terms of the phenomenon that it is a strong company with good performance, but what values and behaviors are inside them. By doing so, we intend to think, implement, and internalize Toyotism as the strongest management technique that is strong in change with our readers, and furthermore, we want to get hints for our company and everyone who works at it to "manage" themselves.

In the first part, we dealt with the "view of work" contained in Toyotism. The fact that the name of the "General Affairs Department" became a "Management Support Team" in the 1990s is a declaration that their paradigm should change, and reveals the need to change the definition of what they have been doing. In that sense, it is possible to understand the paradigm of Toyotism by looking at what Toyota and Lean Companies define and their perspectives on their work.

Part 2 introduces the characteristics of the organization's operations as a means of achieving goals and objectives from the perspective of how Toyota and Lean Companies are doing their jobs. In addition, it introduces the reasons for solving problems and fostering human resources through tasks, and methodologies such as the means and culture that enable them.

In Part 3, we will look at a new aspect of 'work' displayed by Lean companies responding to the challenges of the times to be solved with the values of Toyotism and Lean. Let's look at the case of a company.

However, before going into the main subject, there is one thing I want to reveal. This is why I insist on the term "Toyotism" instead of the term "Lean" already named and known to some extent in the United States.

The first reason is that the level of mindset and working style of Toyota Motor Company and its partners that we can see in close Japan is far higher than that of Lean companies active in the United States, Canada, Australia and Europe. It is the same reason that there is no reason to study the original as a translated version of the original that it is not necessary to use the theory or terminology that was born and developed in Japan. I solidified that idea by reading The Toyota Way by Professor Jeffrey Liker K., published in 2004. Professor Jeffrey said that the results of 20 years of researching and looking at the Lean Company in the United States and Australia were grouped into a book. However, the level of Lean Company he described was considerably lower than that of Toyota Motor Company and its partners in Japan at the time. And this is also the fact that I first confirmed when I toured the Toyota Kentucky plant and its partners in the United States to educate American managers at the Samsung semiconductor plant in Austin in 2004. And, in fact, I also thought that the term Lean method itself was a product of American defeatism. The term Lean is the result of a comparative study of 90 automobile manufacturing plants and Toyota plants in 17 countries around the world for five years from 1986. In 1991, two professors JP Womack and DT Jones called the 'revolution of production methods'. It became known when the word 'Lean Production' was first used in the book. However, that period was when the pride confrontation between the two countries reached its peak, such as when the United States suffered a tremendous recession and American workers who lost their jobs demolished Japanese cars and protested, and in Japan a book titled "Japan Can Say No" came out. It was also. At this time, they would not have been able to call Toyota's name Toyota. So instead, the term lean was used, and it spread all over the world. However, in the sense of returning it to its original place, I would like to save the name of "Toyotism," which Professor Womack should have used.

Second, this is also the reason why this is more important, in order to emphasize "Toyotism" as a concept that contrasts with "Fordism" in the industrial era that encompasses the tasks of the times. Unlike techniques and methodologies that flicker countless times in the flood of words 'revolution' and 'paradigm shift', which are so commonly used, Fordism and Toyotism acted as a paradigm representing the 20th and 21st centuries. I hope you understand.

Now, from now on, let's dive into a new paradigm, "Toyotism," which will solve the challenges of the new era in earnest.

PART 1.

Toyotism, a different perspective on work

In Part 1, we will deal with the "view of work" contained in Toyotism. The person who expressed the source of the Japanese manufacturing industry's competitiveness in terms of ``monozukuri" (made of goods) and melted the idea of the Toyota production method to create the ``characteristic of Japanese manufacturing industry" as a concept that contrasts with the ``world" He is Professor Takahiro Fujimoto of the University of Tokyo.

I will explain in Part 1 that Toyota Motors and other Japanese companies are very different. However, by applying the concept that Professor Fujimoto 'generalizes' the special case of Toyota Motor Company as 'Japanese', I would like to explain how he looks at work.

As for each definition of labor, task, and work, it seems like a topic that many people cannot think deeply about even though they are working on a daily basis.

In this part, you will find answers to the definition of them, the meaning of management that enhances sustainability, and the philosophy of work that focuses on problem solving.

Chapter 1.

Japan's failure, Toyota's success

In this chapter, we want to help you understand how Toyota's view of work differs from other industries and companies. In addition, I would like to explain the "definition of work" that encompasses all industries beyond the scope of the manufacturing industry of Toyota Motor Company and the "recognition that leads to the way of work" that encompasses all sectors.

American-style management vs. Toyota-style management

First, let's start with a story about Japan.

There is a book called The Knowledge-Creating Company. The concept of "Knowledge Management," advocated by the author, Professor Ikujiro Nonaka of Hitotsubashi University, caused a great repercussion in Japan at the time of publication. I have also translated a book called The Leadership of Winners written by Prof. Nonaka et al. Prof. Nonaka's theory of knowledge creation, known as the advocate and master of knowledge management, has spread beyond Japan and around the world.

As Prof. Nonaka pointed out in his book, certainly Japanese companies have made profits through knowledge. Originally, people were the only resource for a Japanese company with no natural resources and high labor costs to succeed. So, there was no better way than converting human work and the knowledge accumulated as a result to profit.

It is true that the litmus, which predicts the tomorrow of developing countries that have grown and developed in a very similar environment and with very similar trajectories, is almost always Japanese. That is why it is necessary to understand what was mediated by Japan's growth. Rather, it is because I believe that Toyota has the correct hints and answers for 'sustainable management' to today's companies, where intellectuals who have studied in the Anglo-American region have a great influence.

To start with the conclusion, American management is a strong methodology for short-range matches. American management is passionate about short-term performance and the performance of a few elites. They appear splendidly and then disappear in an instant. They seem to be interested in the perpetuation of 'management', but not the perpetuation of the 'company' and the 'people' living in it.

On the other hand, Toyota Motor Company's management has many attributes of sustainable management that all global companies must pursue. There are many things that show the achievements that a company that does its essence honestly in a consistent principle, rather than a splendid transformation, can achieve. It has maintained a culture that values the development of a long-term and stable company and the teamwork of the people working in it.

However, the reason why I say that one side is American-style management and the other is "Toyota-style management" rather than Japanese-style management is because most Japanese companies are different from Toyota. Therefore, it is an error to call Toyota's management method Japanese management. And what I basically want to talk about in this book is not just the "method" of companies, but also includes the stories of the "work" of individuals that enable sustainable management. So I heard a flower called Toyota, but in fact, it is my wish as an author that it would be an opportunity to gain insight into the branches and roots that blossomed, that is, people and the "work" they do. Fortunately, the core concepts of Toyotism were accepted by companies such as Amazon and Google and started to blossom in the United States, and other companies are trying to look closely at them.

However, as Japanese management consultant Takao Sakai pointed out in his book The Age of Talents, reading any of the world-renowned Professor Nonaka's books does not clearly explain the relationship between 'knowledge and interest', which is an interest. However, in order to say that profits are created through human 'work', it is necessary to clarify the 'relationship between knowledge and profits' in some way. In that respect, it is worth considering what Sakai explains as follows, based on the theory of production management by Professor Takahiro Fujimoto of the Faculty of Economics at the University of Tokyo.

Toyotism, which recognizes people as a source of profit

In order to explain how knowledge leads to profit and how human labor leads to profit, we must first understand 'labor', 'task' and 'work' separately. First of all, labor means that humans do something using the brain or body. A task is a role in an organization, such as a company, and refers to the unit or process of work assigned to the working person. Finally, work refers to whether or not the result of the labor has produced the expected performance.

In the end, we can say that we did 'work' only when performance was created by performing a given task through labor. And, the work at this time soon becomes profitable. This is the distinction between "work" and "movement" that Toyota emphasizes so much.

Understanding how people and their knowledge have contributed to profits through each era is a very important concept for companies to see people as sources of profit. Because, unlike what is commonly heard, people are always perceived as 'cost'.

As everyone admits, maintaining a person or organization costs money. So, from an accounting point of view, "humans" dealt with in financial accounting are treated only as "expenses" accounts of the same labor costs regardless of the quality or type of work he exerts. In the same way, the "personnel" in management accounting is simply regarded as the labor cost of the person working in the factory or the person working in the office. Or, since regular employees are classified as fixed expenses and dispatched employees as variable expenses, human beings are simply 'costs' in the financial statements regardless of the person and the "work" they perform.

"Our company considers people our greatest asset. Therefore, they are called talent," but when restructuring, there are many companies that mechanically dismiss in the order of higher cost and higher salary. They abuse the word talent according to their tastes as needed. Sometimes it's an asset, sometimes it's just an expense. It's not about a specific company. For managers who are most sensitive to numbers, this is the mechanism by which the unconscious in economics or business administration works.

Also, even though it is a talent, it has not been clearly explained about what exactly it is an asset. In fact, this ambiguity is the same not only in accounting, but also in economics and business administration. Perhaps this is because the background of the birth of these disciplines presupposes the simple labor of the 19th century, that is, manual labor in looking at human "labor". Economics, which refers to the three elements of production, land, labor, and capital, has stopped time in the 19th century. After all, the qualitative aspect of the values humans create through labor could not have been considered at that time. I understand enough. In business administration, which was born afterwards, management was added to land, labor, and capital as the four elements of production. In the textbook, it was described that labor comprehensively refers to all physical and mental labor, land encompasses all infrastructure, and capital encompasses the entire means of production. It seems to be insufficient to follow.

On the one hand, there has always been the idea that working hard with sweat should be respected, whether it is manual labor or mental labor. The amount of labor, or time, has been regarded as an important management resource. On the one hand of such interest in the amount of labor, interest in the quality of work gradually increased, and these were the things that the Japanese have actively promoted after World War II.

'Let's use our brains to see how we can get the same result without sweating less'. The 'improvement' of work, a product of Japanese efforts, is now accepted around the world under the name 'Kaizen'. Furthermore, today, it is not uncommon for people to continue to produce products only with machines and robots without even sweating a single drop. In the end, as can be easily understood, human sweating labor has been replaced by technology, which is the result of professional knowledge. Many countries around the world are enjoying material prosperity due to the labor of 'use your head to get rid of sweaty labor.' This trend was dubbed "Japanese management" by Peter F. Drucker, and it was true that many companies benchmarked Japanese companies.

The fall of other Japanese companies that failed to turn knowledge into work

Then, how should we understand today in Japan, where it is not excessive even if it is expressed as "fall"? As we all know, companies that have enjoyed a period of time, such as Sanyo, NEC, and Matsushita, have lost their competitiveness after the burst of the bubble, and most Japanese companies now belong to the losers. Lifetime employment has completely disappeared in the electronics industry, which has been defeated in the global competition. Workers who thought they would work at one company for their entire life were notified of dismissal. Uh, uh! In the meantime, the company, business units, and factories disappeared. Originally, they are people who have worked hard with the word "economic animals" as the spirit of supporting the Japanese economy. Why did it? Why do Japanese people who have applied the skills and knowledge that enable them to perform tasks more efficiently in their work continue to fail until the end of 30 years? On the other hand, why is Toyota winning and winning even in the same environment?

Here we need to once again understand the relationship

between knowledge and profit. Japan, which once used knowledge to dominate the world, is far from being a leader in knowledge management advocated by Professor Nonaka, but most companies are concentrated in the losers. This is because knowledge or intellectual property has not been converted into a "work" that generates sales or profits.

Think about it. How do people want what they want, whether it be a product or a service, made? For example, why do 'Zara', 'Google' and 'Toyota' succeed, but why did other companies fail? It certainly depends on understanding what a 'selling' product or service is. It is not a matter of state-of-the-art technology, money, or quality in factories that make products. Globally, these indicators are no longer a key source of competitiveness. The battles over what people want, the value created by the goods or services we create and the quality of the "work" that produce performance, have transformed the game into a very different form.

In the modern sense, it is necessary to properly understand what is the value or added value that humans must create, what is the labor that creates it, and what is the relationship between it and corporate interests. It is this lack of awareness that Japanese companies fail today. It's not about technology, talent, or money. Unlike Toyota, their failure is because their thoughts on talent and their "work" are out of date. It is also true that the performance of many Japanese companies such as electricity, telecommunications, and IT seems to have recovered recently. However, in fact, the reality of Japanese companies' resurgence is not "natural recovery," but "artificial recovery" due to the economic stimulus measures artificially created by Abenomics or the Japanese government's budget. Meanwhile, only Toyota Motor Company is commanding the world and sounding the trumpet of self-recovery and advancement. Toyota showed the highest performance in history in the financial results in 2014. That is, sales of 27 trillion 2345 billion yen (about 247 trillion won) and operating profit of 2.75 trillion yen (about 25 trillion 1170 billion won). Surprisingly, looking at the contents, the amount of effect from cost reduction reaches 1.8 trillion yen. Even now, when the world economy was destroyed by COVID19, Toyota Motor Corp. continues its surplus. Toyota's fiscal year 2019 sales amounted to 29,929.9 billion yen. Operating profit was also recorded at 2,442.8 billion yen. Toyota sold a total of 1,045,6593 units in the global market. It is the world's largest car seller. What separated Toyota from other Japanese companies?

Japanese companies certainly had technology, talent, and money. However, since competition in the global market intensified, the existence of Japanese companies has become small enough to be ignored. One of the reasons is that the 'non-sold products' developed and completed by talented individuals with high academic background, technical prowess, and high-level knowledge were produced and managed with the Toyota Production System (TPS), known as the best production system.

The basics of Toyota's production system are to produce 'what is sold' at 'when it is sold' and 'only as much as the amount sold'. Many Japanese companies who did not understand the word of making "sellable products" and tried to sell "made products" as before had to sit in the losers camp. It is 'Galapagos Island, Japan' to express it in a simple way. As far as they are not sold, they still have the world's best source and application technologies.

It is said that the era of mass production is over. Now is the age of overflowing goods. The background is 'the maturity of the market and production technology'. Consumers' eye level has risen because the daily necessities can be obtained both in high quality and inexpensively. Customers pay money only when a product or service that meets their needs is provided. If it fits their needs, they buy a little expensive, but if it doesn't fit their needs, they don't open a wallet, no matter how cheap.

Many companies, such as large corporations that are attracting attention from emerging countries including China, and Apple and Samsung, which are doing business on the global stage, are still making and selling products through mass production. Nevertheless, when I dare say that the era of mass production is over, it means that from the standpoint of companies, the era of supply shortages than demand is over. The reason the society is overflowing with goods and supply is because mass production technology has been established. In the end, it means that the technology related to 'how to make good things cheaper' has greatly evolved over the past 60 years, and that it is no longer a constraint on business whether to secure mass production technology in the manufacturing industry.

As is well known, the mass production system was established by Ford of America. The so-called Ford production system has spread not only to the automobile industry, but also to food processing, beverages, pharmaceuticals, materials, and agriculture. For people it has been common sense for the past 100 years. Everyone sold what they made, and when they made, the product was sold.

However, the production system that Ford is adopting at its factories today is not the Ford production system, but the Toyota production system. Today's Ford is trying to produce only 'as much as what is sold' at 'when it is sold'. They are not selling what they have made, they are making what has already been sold.

Looking back, companies that are booming today are spending the most money on making "what" because their production technology has been established, that is, there are no constraints on how to make it. This is because the company can only make a profit after having such a 'sellable' product. Toyota's track record is because the people in charge of the development process for "sellable things" and the production process that can make it "when sold, as much as the amount sold" performed their labor brilliantly through a given task.

Like this, they are different from the way they look at work.

Chapter 2.

Paradigm change and understanding of world affairs

To know the circumstances of the world. It means that you need to know something to understand how the world works from a different angle. There is a term called paradigm to describe understanding of the world. First of all, we need a basic understanding of what the paradigm is.

What is a paradigm?

To understand the paradigm, I think it is easier to look into the past than to talk about today and the future. This is because people can honestly understand thoughts without prejudice or prejudice when they hear stories of the past that are not directly related to them. Let's understand the paradigm through the story of Emperor Chiyou of Korea and Yellow Emperor of China.

Sima Qian's Records of the Grand Historian has a record of the Yellow Emperor.

"Because of the decline of the country, the princes not only quarreled with each other, but also trampled the people fiercely, but the emperor was unable to grasp it. At this time, the Yellow Emperor defeated them by force, and everyone came and obeyed.

(syncopation)

The Yellow Emperor reigned with this, strengthening the soldiers' power, controlling the rain, the sun, the heat, the wind and the wind, and treating the people by planting five grains: rice, sorghum, barley, millet, and beans."

Meanwhile, there is also a record about Chiyou in the Tang Dynasty records.

"Chiyou obtained the gold of Laoshan and made five weapons."

Also, the records of the Tang Dynasty said this.

"Before the regent of Yellow Emperor, Chiyou had 81 brothers, who spoke human words to the beast's body, had a copper head, iron forehead, and ate sand and stone. They made weapons such as swords, spears, and large bows, and stood out in the world."

Taken together, the situation is like this.

Numerous quarrels arose in the middle of the Yangtze River and the Yellow River, and the history has a deep root. It is easy to understand that farming culture began in the Neolithic era, and there was a power struggle among the settlers. Such confusion can be understood as the Yellow Emperor overpowered by force and brought stability. In short, the Yellow Emperor's power would have been the most well-used tribe of stone weapons in the Neolithic period. It can be said that there was no one to overcome with stone tools. He encompasses the surrounding tribes and secures the position of the chief.

However, it was the emergence of Chiyou, the leader of the Dong Yi tribe, that cast a shadow of crisis on him. Chiyou's army, made of five weapons of metal and armed with metal helmets and armor, must have been recognized by the Yellow Emperor as a monster. Beasts that eat sand and stones. To them the Yellow Emperor was defeated. The second battle, the third battle. The Yellow Emperor lost 73 battles until he lost the final war, Battle of Zhuolu.

Chinese sources say that Yellow Emperor finally wins over Chiyou Emperor, while Korean sources say that

Chiyou Emperor wins, and Yellow Emperor surrenders, but by recognizing his sovereignty, Han Chinese autonomy begins in the middle of the circle. I followed the latter. Because the record always leaves a "trace" whether it recorded true or false. The description of the Chinese librarian as "a head made of bronze, a forehead made of iron" shows that Chiyou Emperor overpowered them by making metal weapons at the time. In addition to this, many traces of him still remain throughout China. The Chinese enshrine Chiyou Emperor as the god of war and build shrines in various places to worship rituals. If Chiyou Emperor was lost in Battle of Zhuolu, and if that is a historical fact, there is no way to explain the collective unconscious that the Chinese still regard Chiyou Emperor as the "god of war". In addition, Koreans still call the highest-ranking people 'Woodu-morri(the head of cow)', which originated from the fact that Chiyou Emperor always wore a bronze helmet on both sides during the war with cow horns on both sides.

Anyway, we can easily understand the paradigm problem in the story of the war between the two. The main paradigm of the Han Chinese-centered society ruled by the Yellow Emperor was stoneware. 'Weapon' meant 'stone weapon'. They couldn't think of anything else, nor did they have to think about it. With that, the Yellow Emperor faction took the place of number one. But something amazing happened. Other forces have pushed in. Moreover, they were using something called a "bronze weapon" that they had not even heard of. Lost in the first battle. Yellow Emperor would have been embarrassed. 'Why did we lose? It's probably because they didn't use stone weapons more efficiently.' Yellow Emperor did not accept the first defeat as a problem with the weapon system. It was accepted as a problem of the efficiency of existing weapons. So in the second and third battles, the Yellow Emperor was defeated. But he still can't change his mind. 'I have been commanding this land with this stone weapon.' Therefore, it was judged that these defeats were a matter of tactics and management. The Yellow Emperor brought more longevity and more troops into war. In 73 battles over 10 years, he lost all of them. Finally, Yellow Emperor surrenders to Chiyou Emperor. Yellow Emperor didn't doubt his paradigm until the end. For him, the weapon system was a stone weapon, and he believed that the victory or defeat of a war depended on tactics and its operation. Such beliefs were not practiced even with the risk of repeated defeats and countless lives. Deciding to surrender, Yellow Emperor was forced to admit that times have changed. Only after he admits that the paradigm has changed will the Bronze Age bloom in mainland China.

If so, what is a paradigm? It refers to the leading 'cognition' that exists in an era or within a group. Larger, it is Zeitgeist, and small, it is 'common sense'. It can be seen that it is a standard of value judgment that is naturally accepted as if breathing. For the people of the age we called the Stone Age, the weapon was stone. Stone still exists today, but today we do not use 'stone' as a means of weapon system. Therefore, the current 'stone' has no meaning at least in the framework of a weapon. What was "all" for them, and "nothing" for us. This is what we call a paradigm. So, what is the paradigm shift that surrounds us today, especially the corporate environment, and how can we reach an understanding of the world to embrace and lead such change? The question naturally proceeds toward understanding the paradigm of our time, that is, the change in world affairs.

In fact, there is a surprising hint about this in the words of understanding the world. The hint is that in order to understand the world, you need to know the relationship between things and information.

I think you can understand all the industries that exist in the world with just this word 'things and information', which will be explained later. The relationship between things and information, or the flow of things and information. To start with the conclusion, we have passed the era when things dominated over the past 100 years, and are entering an era in which information dominates. It means that we are living in a time of paradigm shift. Only humans in the transition period experience a paradigm shift and suffer confusion. People who lived in the middle of the Stone Age do not undergo a paradigm shift. People who lived in the middle of the Bronze Age also do not undergo a paradigm shift. Only those who live in the transition period from the Stone Age to the Bronze Age are confronted with the paradigm problem. In that sense, we are all transitioners of the paradigm shift.

Humans have always struggled with want. There is a general expression that simplifies the process of overcoming such deficiencies. This is Alvin Toffler's distinction. The 'Neolithic Revolution', which is represented by the agricultural revolution, is the first, the 'mass production revolution', which is represented by the industrial revolution, is the second, and finally, the information revolution. It is today's 'knowledge-driven society'.

It took millions of years to fill a hungry stomach. Considering that the world enjoyed the material abundance of today through the industrial revolution that flourished in Europe, it was only about 60 years after World War II. Considering the industrial revolution, it was only 230 years ago. However, the material growth achieved by mankind during that period became the basis of the paradigm of our time. A mindset based on mass production got us to this point. The history of production, which makes things, was the basic driving force in modern society. It was an era where so-called things dominate the world.

From labor to task, from task to work

Marx saw that only human labor can create value. If such labor does not mean only "manual labor", it is somewhat correct. However, this is not true in that the value does not necessarily come true just because there was labor. Once again, human labor (mental labor, which includes not only manual labor of workers, but also labor of white-collar managers, management of managers, and political actions of politicians) is an input factor. The process, or process, of producing something, that is, goods or services with such inputs, is a 'task'. Even at this stage, it cannot be said that value or added value is necessarily generated. This is the reason why we should assume that we have done 'work' only when we achieve the result that such labor and tasks have actually created some value or added value. So, in the previous chapter, I explained that it was necessary to distinguish between labor, task, and work, and it was also said that "work" in Toyota refers to only the moment when value or added value occurs as work. The rest are non-valued work or non-value added work.

In the end, human labor is transformed into a 'work' that creates new value or added value through a process led by a 'task' given according to their role, whether it is farming, working in a factory, processing information in the office, or anguish of managers. When it is done, it is meaningful. This determines the relationship between 'knowledge and profit', which was described in the previous chapter.

The interest in business administration, in a word, only reflects the expansion of the proportion from labor to task and from task to work. What does this mean?

Alvin Toffler categorized the whole history of mankind as the first wave (agricultural revolution), the second wave (industrial revolution), and the third wave (information revolution). Peter Drucker divided the history after the Industrial Revolution into industrial revolution, productivity revolution, and management revolution. Now we all describe our time in terms of knowledge revolution or information revolution. These are all good symbols that reveal the challenges of the times.

First of all, the task of the times of the industrial revolution was in the 'mass production' itself. In the term of the Productivity Revolution, it is said that the "efficiency" of how to make mass production with few resources, how much, and how fast was the task of the times. The management revolution, the information revolution, and the knowledge revolution are now revealing that it is the task of the times to decide the 'What' beyond the age of 'how'. In other words, the question of what to do, what to make, and what is different or new?

You must have understood how the center of worries has changed from "labor" (input) to "task" (process), and from "task" (process) to "work" (performance).

Let's take a look at how this flow of knowledge was applied to solve the challenges of each era, and how it secured the interests of leading companies of that era by process.

Realization of mass production (head to hand)

It is not necessary to talk about the trend of the Western era, but it can be easily understood through the development history of Korea that has successfully undergone industrialization in a relatively short period.

Under the plan called "Five-Year Economic Development Plan," which began in 1962, the so-called educational policy to achieve early industrialization focused on fostering skilled workers. The industrial revolution of the Republic of Korea, which succeeded to the agricultural state of Joseon, was also the result of the 770,000 high school students who were nurtured during this period. Compulsory elementary school education was a good means to supply people who could read and write to factories.

In the early industrialization society, as in Korea, in Europe, and in the United States, the influx of rural populations into cities and inexpensive labor was demanded. In other words, it was necessary to cultivate a large number of workers with educational background and skills enough to understand instructions and read standardized manuals. They were the protagonists of the "industrial revolution" that enabled the explosive supply of goods. The knowledge needed to move the hand effectively was enough. It demanded that all human capacities go to the fingertips. Knowledge of this period flowed into the hand, and increasing the input determined the output. (head to hand)

The pursuit of efficiency (head to head) and the birth of management

In the preface of a book entitled 《Samsung, a History of Persistent Innovation》, written by Professor Wook Son from Samsung, the following expression is found.

"Innovation is the introduction of the most advanced methodology to achieve results and shape. By doing so, we can create a competitive advantage that creates customer value better, cheaper, and faster."

There's no way competitors won't show up in a time when you make money just by making things. As competitors began to participate in the market, the task of the company's times shifted to pursuing efficiency in mass production. Efficiency, as Professor Wook Son said, is making it better, cheaper, and faster. A 'methodology' was needed to solve this.

The theme of Korea's first seminar to improve efficiency was 'Material Management'. The instructor of the material management seminar held on August 13, 1962 was an instructor at the Army Logistics School. It is easy to understand that the terms and methodologies of early management were borrowed from the military. In 1976, the Management Training Program (MTP), a manager training program initiated by the US Air Force, was introduced, and TWI (Training Within Industry) was introduced as a supervisor training program for on-site work guidance and management.

Until the 1970s, the world economy experienced rapid growth and was sold as it was made. For that reason, many companies that have taken the advantage of strong export-drive policies have focused on quantitative growth in order not to be pushed out of the trend of growth. In the meantime, the US, which had been at its forefront, suffered two oil shocks, giving Japan the lead. In order to overcome this, the methodologies developed by US companies and the methodologies used by Japanese companies that have become number one are introduced to the world one after another.

Value engineering (VE), proposal activities, total quality control (TQC), total production innovation (TPI), total productive maintenance (TPM) for cost reduction With the introduction one after another, from the late 1980s, companies entered the heyday of so-called management innovation. Throughout this period, many companies shift their interest in product to the process in which the product is released. Without solving this task, they couldn't make better products cheaper and faster. All knowledge was focused on efficiency in securing competitive advantage. Knowledge of this period flowed through the head.

The task of the times in this period was securing the

rationality of the function, quality and price of own products. With the advent of competitors making the same product, customers who have broadened options have opened their wallets to companies that offer convincing quality, functionality, and price. So-called head to head. It was a time when all the capabilities had to be put together to convince customers, and this was the result of minimizing the loss and defects in the process of getting their products out. On June 7, 1983, Samsung Chairman Kunhee Lee's job, "Change everything except your wife and children," was a historic event that clearly presented the challenges of the times and suggested the principle of action to value quality in the product making process.

A time when people must move their hearts (head to heart)

And finally now, the Republic of Korea has somehow succeeded in catching up with Western advanced countries. However, it also means that from an industrial perspective, it is time to hand over the leadership of the secondary industry to other countries such as China. Like advanced western countries. Developed countries, often referred to as OECD member countries, are already living in reality with the highest proportion of tertiary industries, even from the present point of view.

The so-called head to heart! This is an era in which all human capabilities must be focused on grasping people's minds, and an era in which people themselves are the subject of innovation. This means the end of the era led by things and entering an era led by information and emotions. It is also a request for a paradigm shift for everyone living in the 21st century.

If the 20th century is an era led by things, it is worth remembering the keyword that the 21st century is an era of information. A product or service is no longer a purpose in itself, but a means for creating customers and creating customer value. In that sense, it is an excellent foresight that Peter Drucker said that the purpose of a company is to "create customers". It would not be wrong to say that the convergence between industries that are not related at all was eventually derived from an attempt to capture the hearts of customers. No matter what job you do, if you don't get "approval from the minds of the customer," that is, if there is no performance in terms of sales or profits obtained by achieving the purpose of the company, it is not "work". Goods or services that are not sold are those whose existence values are not recognized.

Chapter 3.

Toyotism, a new insight into work

After all, our past shows how the relationship between things and information, or the superiority of things and information, has changed. This means that no matter what industry, what kind of industry you are in, you can describe your work as a basic principle.

Take a look at the following picture. This is a picture from 《Introduction to Production Management》 by Professor Takahiro Fujimoto of the Faculty of Economics at Tokyo University, a renowned researcher of Toyota production methods.

He explains that the core of production management, that is, the core of Monozukuri in Japanese, is 'to create a good flow of design information from product development (design) to purchase, production, and sales.' Professor Fujimoto used the concept of 'design information' to describe the manufacturing industry, but here he intends to expand the scope and use the term 'ideal information' as a concept that applies to all industries. The word ideal information was chosen from the meaning of 'information containing the most ideal state that a product or service wants to achieve'.

All industries are the creation and transcription process of ideal information.

Ideal information is the outcome created through processes such as investigation, planning, development, and design. For example, for products in the assembly industry such as computers and automobiles, the elements that form the product's attractiveness or value, such as the results of R&D or technology development, and the exterior and interior design, are literally included. It becomes standard information and is transmitted to the production preparation department or factories around the world. In addition, in the process industry such as steel, glass, and chemical products, or in the material industry, information describing the manufacturing process is ideal. In the service industry, for example, McDonald's values and manuals are considered the most desirable through their business, and the unit of knowledge and information to realize it can be called ideal information.

Simply put, it would be nice to understand it as a recipe

for cooking. In other words, ideal information is the processing knowledge and information necessary and sufficient to create products and services of the required quality.

This ideal information largely entails two processes. One is the process of creating the information, and the other is the process of transcribing and copying the information as it is, that is, the process of transcription.

First of all, whether it is new business development or product development, what is actually performed upstream of work can be said to be 'creating ideal information'. On the other hand, even if we hear the news that a new technology has been developed, we cannot have the product right away. This is because only when mass production technology is secured, mass production and supply can be made to the world. In that case, manufacturing and production means making copies of this "ideal information" in the end. Transcription refers to the copying of text or pictures as they are, and the manufacturing process that must ensure reproducibility and repeatability is literally the process of reproducing ideal information and repeating it. In other words, we call 'quality' in other words, how well these warriors implement ideal information. Quality inspection is nothing more than this measure of reproducibility and repeatability.

The task of the times at the beginning of the industrial revolution was "mass production" itself. Companies that succeeded in reproducing and repeating the product as it was in the ideal information were able to eat honey from the early industrial revolution days. The industry that represented the industry was manufacturing, and companies and countries that performed well in this transcription process were able to blow the trumpet of growth. As we are well aware, securing mass-production technology and leading economic growth through it has been transferred from Europe, the home of the Industrial Revolution, to the United States and then to Japan, and now Asia, including Korea and China, has. The center of 'transcription' ability is now in Asia.

However, this is not the case when considering whether the industries of advanced countries such as Europe and the United States, which have passed the flag of growth to emerging countries including Korea and China, have been eliminated. It is also true that advanced countries that have surrendered the superiority of the manufacturing industry are creating tremendous value and added value based on the tertiary industry based on the space and time of globalization, digitalization, and information. Still they are in the lead.

In that way, no matter how globalization progresses and the earth is flat, the world is not yet the same. Many countries still have the highest share of primary industries, some countries have secondary industries at the center of the national economy, and some have an overwhelmingly high share of tertiary industries, such as developed countries. The number of scenarios and cases for which strategies and tactics should be taken according to this stage of development is so numerous that we may now be replacing the mess with the word "complex system".

But what if there is one basic principle that runs through all these industries and you can understand it?!

This is one of the basic principles.

'All industries in the world are the creation and/or transcription of ideal information.'

The primary industry is literally transcribing the genetic information of crops to obtain the same fruits and seeds. The secondary industry is the transcription of design drawings as processed knowledge, that is, ideal information through medium (materials). The same goes for the tertiary industry. The reason we can see the growth of companies such as McDonald's, Disneyland and the Ritz-Carlton Hotel is that their ideal information (a manual that covers mission, vision, and service in general) is used by the frontline employees (medium), although they This is because even non-regular workers such as part-time jobs or contract workers are recreated and repeatedly transcribed with the same service at any store in the world. The primary industry is to reproduce genetic information as given in nature, while the secondary industry is to artificially reproduce ideal information conceived by human imagination or needs. In addition, the tertiary industry can be understood in terms of embodiing and transcribing the human concept through humans themselves, not other objects or materials.

In this way, all industries can be said to be the creation and transcription of ideal information. The creation of the ideal information and the result of transcription are called quality. Quality is not only the quality of crops or products, but also the concept to provide human-provided services, and how much the transcription activities have satisfied the needs of buyers.

Let us understand that all working humans spend their day in the process of creating ideal information or transcribing the created ideal information. Then we may be able to understand today's complex-looking global village amid the vertical flow of 230 years since the Industrial Revolution and the horizontal aspect of space where the gap between the rich and the poor and the imbalance between industries still appear.

The task of creating ideal information can be called a value task, and the task of transcribing abnormal information can be called a value-added task.

The difference between Fordism and Toyotism in terms of looking at work

Corporate activities active in all industries can be summarized as a process that produces results that satisfy customers through the task of 'creating ideal information or transcription'. From this point of view, I think that Toyota is the first company to awaken that "labor" as an input element should be the "work" that creates the most value and added value through the "task" as a process. In order to do that, I will also explain the fact that it is necessary to eliminate the value-added work and that Toyota is the company that has the most experience and know-how about it. In that sense, I would like to emphasize the importance of Toyotism.

After all, work is managing labor and tasks so that you can achieve results. From this point of view, Fordism or Toyotism can be applied to any job regardless of all types of business, and the status of "general theory" can be obtained. Because they are both talking about 'the perspective and way of looking at work'. A comparison of the paradigms for work between Fordism and Toyotism is as follows.

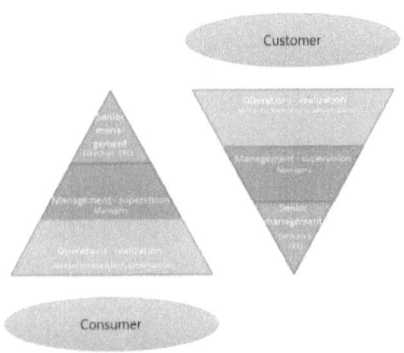

Fordism has managers at the top of a pyramidal organization. And the concept is that there are consumers who consume the goods and services supplied at the bottom. Unlike customers, the word consumer is also a very passive and passive concept. As is often said, the pyramid structure is the most stable structure. Nevertheless, it is not anxiety but distrust that managers feel anxious. So, when the economy is not improving or the performance is not good, it is to restructure the underperformer and underperforming organizations. So-called "organizational innovation". There is a hidden paradigm that blames managers and sub-employees who do not properly carry out their will, rather than reflection on the intentions of managers and management.

On the other hand, Toyotism is a perspective that puts the origin of activities on the customer. Now that the employees are doing well, the organization does not collapse or fall, but the inverted pyramid structure that always looks unstable makes managers anxious. It is different from distrust of members. This kind of anxiety that the sword may fall from above at any time makes it possible to understand the meaning of the adage, "Whoever wants to wear a crown, bear its weight."

The CEO realizes that in order to eliminate such anxiety, it is necessary to identify and nurture avant-garde employees who can design and transcribe correct ideal information by identifying customer needs. And they start to try to provide opportunities and fields to maximize their abilities. It is so-called "organizing innovation".

So, understanding the paradigm of Toyotism has the same meaning as understanding the contemporary task of the present era. When the origin of ideal information design matches the needs of customers, companies and organizations can achieve great results.

An era where the creation of ideal information becomes money

Business activities have been called 'the process of creating ideal information and transcribing it'. If you think about this a little bit, corporate activities can be broadly divided into 'the process of creating ideal information' and 'the process of transcribing ideal information'.

However, it is now common sense that the process of creating ideal information creates far more profits. The more developed countries and the more people who create ideal information within a company, the higher the profit and income.

Let me give you a very easy example.

The following phrase is engraved on many Apple products, including the iPhone.

"Designed by Apple in California Assembled in China"

This means that it is Apple's headquarters in California that creates the intrinsic value of ideal information, the outcome of planning, design, and development, and the assembly was done in China. In other words, it means that the labor of Apple employees was used to create the ideal information, and the labor of Chinese company employees such as Foxconn was put into the transcription of the ideal information. We all know that most of the profits go to Apple. This means that most of the profits come from the process of 'creating ideal information', not from the process of 'transcription'. In other words, it means that the value of creating something from nothing (creating ideal information) is more profitable than the added value (transcription of ideal information) that creates something from the thing. At first glance, consumers seem to buy a product, but in reality they are buying ideal information, that is, value. The emergence of 3D printers, which is drawing attention in recent years, clearly shows that in the future, we will not pay to purchase the product, but pay to buy the blueprint of the product.

This trend can be applied not only to the manufacturing industry but also to the service industry. The source of competition for companies like Disney and Starbucks is their information assets, or ideal information. According to Hiroshi Kamata, our advisor and author of The Disney Series, which sold 1 million copies in Japan, Disney employees are trained to provide the same service anytime, anywhere. In addition, Disney's original products are said to have uniform dimensions and materials for even doll. This is because random service or randomly designed dolls destroy Disney's values. It means that standards are strictly set and managed from products to employees so as not to be hindered by the realization of their mission of providing happiness to all who come. Disneyland of dreams and fantasy is being transcribed through their employees and products based on standardized ideal information (mission, vision, principle of action, manual, etc.).

At McDonald's and Starbucks stores all over the world, we can expect the same experience, and we actually experience it. The fake Louis Vuitton bag, which can be purchased for $20 at the Guangzhou fake market, is cheap because it is not transcribed in the right way with the ideal information (brand, idea) of the original brand. However, the original Louis Vuitton bags produced in Chinese factories provide a high level of social status that cannot be obtained with the material and sewing alone, and they also generate high profits. No matter where these stores are located or where they are sold in any country, it is obvious that most of the revenue goes to the head office with the ideal information. And, as we know, the head offices of such companies usually exist in developed countries. It will be a good answer to what kind of work the people of developed countries should do.

As seen above, the biggest asset, whether it be manufacturing or service, must be an information asset called ideal information. And the value of this ideal information is obtained as the result of R&D, designer's design, and intellectual activity such as integrated circuit design. The market is showing that the transcription of ideal information is not enough now, thanks to the advancement of the production technology to make the product itself and the manufacturing technology related to how efficiently it will be produced as we pass through the era of things. .

This is why I try to explain 'Toyotism' as an idea and methodology that not only those working in the manufacturing industry, but rather those who work in support organizations such as the office and development sectors or in the process of creating ideal information.

A new perspective on work,

From input to output

It was called 'work' that human labor creates performance through tasks. In other words, a labor or task that does not produce performance has no meaning. You shouldn't think you've done your job just because you went to work or followed a given process. That may be why, but it is also true that there are overflowing discussions and books about how to do a job well. However, in order to do 'work' that produces performance, it will be necessary to understand what it is.

All humans do is create ideal information and its transcription. Just as all industries say the creation and transcription of ideal information, all human labor can be reduced to labor that creates ideal information (creation-type labor) and labor that transcribes ideal information to medium and services (transcription-type labor). . If you want to do your job well, you need to be aware of what kind of work you are doing. Even if a person in charge of creation-type labor eagerly implements the methodology of transcription-type labor, or if a person in charge of transcription-type labor practices the methodology of creation-type labor to die, the performance cannot be good.

After all, we, you and I, are the ones in charge of either. Either we are in charge of creative labor or transcription-type labor. Recognizing the effective methodology for each type of work, through this, it is to change it into a 'work' that produces performance in the 'task' of carrying out one's own 'labor'.

The process of inputting and outputting through the process and the required capabilities are as follows.

Skill, or skill, is the ability to do the job. But just as you need to get a driver's license to become a driver, knowledge can help you do the job better. In other words, knowledge combined with experience can lead to extraordinary performance and ultimately better output. Attitude is the more fundamental thing you need to do a better job, it can do it excellently, and it can make it a chore. Confucius' wisdom that "the acquaintance is not limited to the ones who like it, and the ones who like it is not only the ones who enjoy it" is valid now and in the future. Work is both a purpose and a means for humans. How it is defined depends on the attitude of the person doing the job.

I once went to lecture at a company in China. A driver came out at Shenzhen Airport and greeted me. When I finished training and headed back to the hotel, it was late after 8pm. The driver seemed to be trying to get me to the hotel as soon as possible, and ran at a faster pace than when I came. I felt that the car was relatively quiet, so I asked the driver about the model of car, and our conversation began.

Following a short answer to my question, he memorized car makers and models in China, and car makers and models in Japan, Korea, Germany, the United States, and France. I was amazed and said, "You're so smart," and he shook his hand saying no and talked about cars for a while. I was deeply impressed and once again said, 'You seem so smart,' and he shook his hand again. So I said, 'I think you really like cars,' and he admitted that. He said that he liked cars, but he didn't have money, so he was very happy to drive a car while working as a driver at a company, and he was very happy to see all the cars in the world on the street. In that sense, he said that the presence of customers who visit his company is the people who allow him to drive himself, so he is serving with all his heart. For four days from that day, I saw the power of "work" achieved by the union of his "task" and "attitude" standing firmly behind his kindness and smile. For a driver who belongs to a company and has to deal with customers, the real job is to make sure that the person visiting the company has a good impression of the company. Anyone who thinks that driving as an input is work can't have this performance. Only those who have a proper definition of the output that should be obtained through my task can do 'work'.

Chapter 4.

Creative Labor and Enterprise Labor, Understanding Values and Added Values

Maximization of value work and value-added work in the Toyota method

The final product of the primary and secondary industries can be expressed as follows.

Product = ideal information + medium (material)

The service, the final product of the tertiary industry, can be expressed as follows.

Service = ideal information + medium (person)

In other words, if manufacturing industry projects the same object on the basis of drawings, reproduces and repeats it, it can be said that the service industry is projected to people based on core values or manuals and reproduced and repeated anytime, anywhere.

As the small ideas of someone or of a team or organization are refined and materialized, values (creating something from nothing) such as a business model or product concept are created. The ideal information created in this way is handed over to the tangible and intangible field for realizing values such as factories and stores. Then, there, the material and the person become the medium for the realization of the ideal information, and by putting in the labor of transcribing it, added value (creating something from existence) is realized in each process. In the end, we call the product or service the result of this completion, and we can say that we 'worked' only when it produced a quality result that satisfies the customer's needs.

Here, we are in charge of one of the labor that creates ideal information, that is, the labor that creates value, and the labor that does transcription, that is, creates added value. Value-creating labor and value-adding labor are performed according to tasks or work processes imposed by each organization. In the end, doing a good job means maximizing the ratio of the time spent creating or transcribing ideal information, while minimizing the time or tasks that are not being created or transcribed.

Isn't there a company that comes to mind here? Yes. It is Toyota Motor Company. In other words, the Toyota method is nothing other than 'the method of thorough exclusion of waste (non-value work, non-value-added work)'.

Manufacturers who have adopted or learned the Toyota method have failed because they do not understand its essence. There may be a reason why the 2009 Toyota recall situation continues and interest in the Toyota method has rapidly cooled. However, it is necessary to pay attention to the recent success of Toyota Motor Company, which has overcome the crisis and is performing the best, and I think the root of it is understanding the core of Toyotism.

Think about it. That is why Japan, the manufacturing kingdom of craftsmanship and cutting-edge processing technology, is collapsing! Japan itself proves that it is not because of a lack of craftsmanship or advanced technology. The performance of strong and winning companies regardless of industry, including Toyota, Google, Amazon, Alibaba, Zara and Uniqlo, is because they removed non-value work among their labor and tasks. In other words, it is the result of discovering and effectively removing non-value and non-value-added work that restrict the creation of value and added value. They thoroughly focused their thoughts and actions on the value and added value that the business has to offer. It can be explained in the strategic terms of selection and concentration, or it can be viewed as a difference in the corporate culture of their companies.

The essential thing is that companies or organizations that create 'good ideal information' that can contribute to society and deliver 'good flow of ideal information' to customers and markets, and such are strong organizations and strong talents.

In the Toyota method, singing 'make one-piece-flow production' and 'make a flow' is the process of creation and transcription of this ideal information, namely, development-design-purchase-production-sales. The best flow in the process, that is, a process that minimizes non-value-added work or non-value-added work should be established.

There are many companies that have neglected the Toyota method because they are different from ours or that we are a service industry, not a manufacturing industry. However, we need to know that this "work" in the Toyota method is the "work" we must pursue. The companies that really realized the difference are Amazon, Google, and Samsung.

Again, just as Ford Motors and Fordism have to be identified, Toyota Motors and Toyotism need to be identified. However, their name remains in history because Ford Motors was the first to open their eyes to the challenges of mass production in the last 100 years and find the solution first. Likewise, in the era of oversupply in the 21st century, we need to look into them and remember them because Toyota Motors is the first to open our eyes to the change in the challenges of the times and find the solution first. Moreover, because that period is now where we live.

In retrospect, Jim Collins' 《Good to Great》 is a book that is born of vulgar anticipation that there will be some secret because of the achievements now, and the price of that expectation is 《How The Mighty Fall: And Why Some Companies Never Give In》. This is why we should not see the flickering star, but the principle beyond it. This is why you should look at the moon instead of looking at your pointing finger. For this reason, I would like you to think that Toyota, which is mainly cited in this book, is merely a synonym for a pioneer who defines and finds solutions to the problems of the times of our time, rather than the actual Toyota cars of Nagoya, Japan. The same is true of the organization or its people.

Toyota first recognized the superiority of information originating from customers

In that sense, all businesses, whether secondary or tertiary, can be called content industries. This is because they create their own business model or design as ideal information, transfer it through media such as materials or people, and deliver it to customers or markets.

Then, in this process, what is the difference between the era of short supply that required mass production in the last century and the era of oversupply today? The flow of goods and information in the last century, centered on the secondary industry, which made contact with consumers or customers through goods, is as follows.

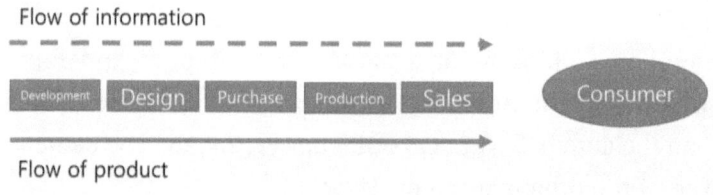

This is why the mass production era is called the supplier-centered era. In times of shortage of goods, business was established with only the services and products provided by suppliers unilaterally. In fact, information doesn't make much sense, and mainly products alone were enough to make money. Business was to sell what you made. And if you actually made it, it was sold. The product produced was value and added value. Since the thought of the supplier becomes a product and flows to the consumer, the flow of information and the flow of the product are the same.

Then, what would be the flow of goods and information in today's age of oversupply?

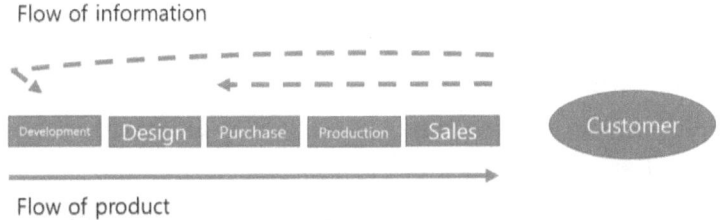

Naturally, oversupply means a sharp competitive environment.

As consumers' choices have expanded, no one can guarantee that our products will be sold right away. Whether you're doing market research or not, it's not that important, anyway, the flow of information to understand customer needs must flow from the market to development. No matter how much intuition and insight is emphasized, it is because, as Kant once said, "Experience without theory is blind, but theory without experience is mere intellectual play." The voice of the customer, that is, VOC, should be the origin of development. Of course there can be objections. Henry Ford, the founder of Ford, a representative company of the past, said that "if we asked consumers what they wanted, they would probably have said "faster horses." Sony's chairman Akio Morita, who created the Walkman, also pushed the Walkman project to success with that logic. Recently, Apple's Steve Jobs also said that consumers know nothing. "When Graham Bell made the phone, did he do market research? I just want innovation." However, when Ford, Sony, and Apple were winning, they were temporarily "only one." As competitors emerged, Ford and Sony fell, and if Apple continued to do this, it surely fell. Realizing that, Apple said that it has too many product lineups for Samsung, and they, who had forced consumers to have only one model, are also on the path of revising their strategy to follow Samsung.

From the standpoint of a consultant who takes 'generalization of special cases' as his profession, I do not want to recommend this path to readers. In the sense of pursuing excellence, Only One is worthwhile, but overall, I don't think it would be desirable for someone to enjoy monopoly profits from 'Only One' products and services forever. That greed broke Wall Street. It is not sustainable.

In that sense, the origin of development should be the market, and the market economy should be based on "goodwill" among various players.

On the other hand, for products currently being produced, the sales information of the customer should be a flow that is directly transmitted to production or purchase. In other words, you should not sell what you made, but make what you have already sold. It is no longer common sense that the life of a restaurant or fast food restaurant is not made in advance, but depends on how quickly the order is made.

As seen above, it is important to recognize that the flow of goods from development to production and sales to consumers has an upper hand, and the time we live in is an era in which information originating from customers has an upper hand. In that respect, Toyota is also the first company to recognize the superiority of "information". So, they introduced a pull method (a build-to-order manufacturing method that produces products according to the flow of information) rather than a push method (a push method by plan). It was in 1953, so it was very fast.

Chapter 5.

Understanding Control and Management

The survival inequality of a company through value

The relationship between the creation of the ideal information, the transcription of the ideal information, and the cost of the medium (human labor or material), as discussed above, is as follows in terms of profit.

Creation of ideal information (value)> Transcription of ideal information (value added)> medium (cost)

This is not necessarily a 'explaining' that the creation (value) of ideal information has a higher profit than the transcription (value added) of the ideal information, and the transcription of the ideal information is more profitable than the medium cost. Rather, in order for a company to survive and make a profit, the creation (value) of ideal information must have a greater profit than the transcription (value added) of the ideal information, and the transcription (value added) of the ideal information must have a greater profit than the cost of the medium to be input. It is an inequation.

In business administration, there is a so-called survival inequation

Value> Price> Cost

It means that the price must be higher than the cost that the company puts in, and the value provided to the customer must be greater than the price in order for the company to survive. This survival inequation seems to be easily explained by the laws of thermodynamics in physics.

The first law of thermodynamics is 'the law of conservation of energy', and the second law of thermodynamics is 'the law of entropy'. The law of entropy, in simple terms, is that available energy turns into unusable energy. When a room with a temperature of 30 degrees and a room with a temperature of 20 degrees are connected to each other, energy moves from the high temperature to the low temperature, and the energy movement stops at 25 degrees. Soon, the available energy turns into an unusable energy state.

Like the laws of thermodynamics in physics, if the value provided by a company is higher than the price and the cost is lower than the price, the customer's enthusiasm for the product or service will not cool down, and will continue to flow in profits toward the enterprise. However, at the point of value = price = cost, energy transfer no longer occurs, and no corporate profit occurs. Needless to say, of course, when value <price <cost, the company disappears. It is obvious that the energy flowing to the company is transferred to competitors or other companies according to the law of energy conservation.

Likewise, when looking at the size of the profits of each industry in terms of industry, the creation of ideal information should be more profitable than the entire company of ideal information, as the tertiary industry> secondary industry> primary industry feels natural. The efficiency of the transfer process should be higher than the media cost. By understanding these basic principles, we can easily agree that one should turn one's labor into "work," keeping in mind the maximization of value or added value in each field.

We must escape from the idea that labor = work or task = work. We can survive and prosper only when we get out of the idea that we are working because we are in a company or that we are working because we are doing something. If we do not have a sense of growth and success in it, when and how can each individual and each person's competitiveness be gained in this era when the concept of lifelong work has disappeared? In academy? English skills? We must grow where we are.

In order for the equation of labor + task = work to be established, it is not a management of the amount of labor input and the amount of work, but a work that generates profits through the quality of the inputted labor, organic integration with the work, and overall optimization. That's why I call for output-centric 'work smart', not input-centric work hard.

In the modern society where the value of human knowledge labor becomes even greater, efforts to improve the "quality" of people, that is, the "quality" of ideal information, must precede. Then we can experience the following inequality.

Creation of ideal information> Transcription of ideal information> Medium cost

Then, let's look at how we can interpret the creation of ideal information and the meaning of the company from the perspective of "management" that we are familiar with and often use.

Both sides of work, must be changed while maintaining

Let's think about the meaning of management.

Again, let's look at the structure of what we do.

Work = Creation of ideal information (value creation) and / or Transcription of ideal information (value-added creation)

Here, first of all, I remember that the transcription of ideal information was defined as the activity of copying and reproducing the determined ideal information as it is. If so, it's easy to understand that basically the purpose of this activity is to set standards and to effectively transcribe while suppressing deviations from these standards. In other words, what the central axis of the activity keeps is in 'maintenance'.

On the one hand, the creation of ideal information is a process of creating something from nothing or transitioning from an existing one to a better one, so it aims to deviate from the existing standards or even out of the existing framework itself. In other words, the central axis of the activity is 'change'.

The viewpoint of creation of ideal information is change and transcription of ideal information is maintained can be applied to the interpretation of management as it is. In simple terms, control has an upper and a lower limit. On the other hand, there is no upper limit to management.

There are upper and lower limits of control, so if the upper limit of control is exceeded, so-called over quality (over quality) is achieved, or if it exceeds the lower limit of control, it becomes defective. Neither is desirable. The state within the range becomes the best. Control is the power to keep and maintain.

However, another meaning in management, although there is a lower limit, there is no upper limit. It is important to tolerate the so-called surprise that transcends the existing framework or common sense and stereotypes in order to create a better result than yesterday, something that did not exist yesterday. Rather, it is management that needs to promote transcending existing lines. Management is about changing and driving change. And if you think of management in the broader sense that includes control, the art of dealing with the functions of fixed and variable can be called management.

Looking at it this way, the roles and jobs of the people we often refer to as the manager and the executive will become clear. It is easier and more clear what the roles of those who are in charge of 'creating ideal information' such as planning, marketing, and development and those who are in charge of 'transcription of ideal information' such as management support, quality assurance, and manufacturing departments. It is recognized. The same is true in terms of empowerment and organizational functions of the company. The people we work with can become the subject of management by clearly knowing whether they should be doing things that make a difference or what they keep.

Understanding that management is a function of fixed and volatile, it is not only the top managers who shout for change and only the managers are supposed to obey the rules. If one side tells you to keep and the other tells you to work creatively, so if you don't know who to listen to, it might be a story that you don't understand the nature of work. Because there is a side to maintain and a side to change in everyone's work. In other words, the work to be maintained and obeyed and the work to be created or changed exist together. Therefore, maintenance and improvement should be taken as equivalent to the two basic aspects of work, the front and back sides of a coin or two wheels of a bicycle. So management is maintenance + improvement.

Toyotism refers to 'work', a continuation of maintenance and improvement

In this way, you can easily understand business activities with the keywords of fixed and variable. When it comes to labor costs, regular workers equivalent to a fixed amount, irregular workers equivalent to a variable amount, or daily or contract workers are used. Also, the creation of ideal information is in charge of regular workers, and the transcription of ideal information is achieved through non-regular workers or part-time jobs. This is the way companies like Apple and Nike are taking. One example of this division of roles is that Apple or Nike is in charge of design and outsourced production to external specialized companies.

In addition, most companies set and fix the amount of production or work to be processed per day, and the fluctuations to it are responded through the number of business days or working days. Likewise, the standard process or standard time is fixed, and it responds to customer changes through the number of stores or lines. If this fixation and change are passive expressions for market conditions or customer response in corporate activities, the above-described maintenance and change can be said to be more active expressions for market creation or customer envelopment.

Toyota understands and does this very clearly. Let's check the concept of work at Toyota that many are familiar with.

Work = maintenance + improvement

This is the definition of this job that is the first concept you learn when you go to Japan to train Toyota Motor Company. They know what was explained earlier. They know that you need to know what 'work' is before doing 'work'. It's something I know, so I think there is a difference in performance as well.

A person who manages himself, that is, a person with self-leadership, can be said to be a person who continues to run the cycle of maintenance + improvement in their work and life. When we say that we often feel rewarded or fulfilled in our work, it is often the time to properly transcribe (maintain) the ideal information and receive recognition from customers. And, when you say you feel that you're growing up in your work, it's when you 'improved' by finding a better way or value for work. After all, as many companies think, 'motivation' is not something a company or a boss can give unilaterally.

However, the company and the boss can only give 'opportunity'. So, in terms of corporate culture, whether you have a perspective of problem solving vertically and horizontally, overall optimization for growth and success, and whether your bosses are interested in the growth of their subordinates becomes a very important factor.

We tend to think that work = maintenance. Since we made additional contributions when we improved, the paradigm of work=maintenance is hidden behind our psychology, which is hoping for something to be rewarded. However, if you look at the process of work, you find that work = maintenance + improvement is a continuation. In the next chapter, we will look at the powerful power of maintenance and improvement through the management cycle to keep things going.

Chapter 6.

Toyota's Philosophy That Reveals Problems

Problems in the existing PDCA cycle

If we look at the concept of work being a continuation of maintenance or improvement, we can understand that a different work cycle is needed than the 'Deming Cycle' we commonly know. This is because there are not so many things to start with 'plan' unless it is a startup.

The figure below shows the PDCA cycle, or a management cycle called the Deming Cycle. In the previous chapter, I explained that management is about maintaining, but as everyone knows, the purpose of management is also a continuous activity that involves moving toward a higher level while maintaining the current level. Therefore, as shown in the figure, on the current standards and standards(Plan), execute it as it is (Do), identify the gap between the plan, execution, and performance (Check), and improve the extracted task

(Act)' is a way to get closer to the target 'desired future status' (DFS, Desired Future Status) as time passes by continuously rotating the cycle. Surprisingly, however, it is true that this cycle, which many people are tired of even if they have nails in their ears, does not work well. This is because it is not difficult to keep running the PDCA cycle. Then, why is it difficult to ensure continuity with the PDCA cycle?

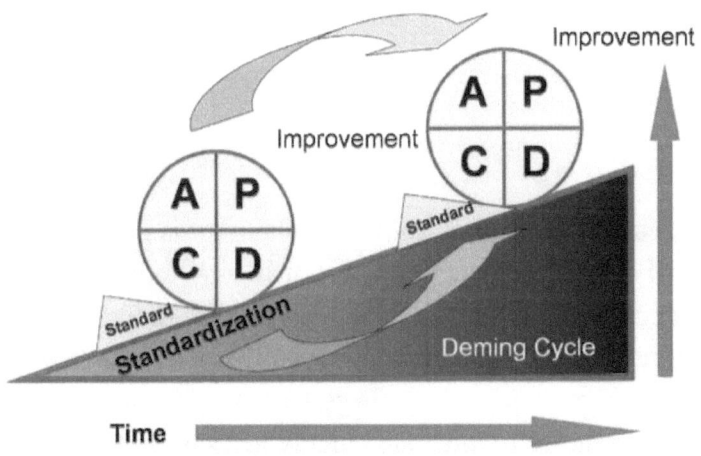

Deming Cycle

It is that the first problem is that the gap between the performance and the gap when executed is large because the PDCA cycle starting from P is often not verified for the plan, that is, the goal itself, due to its nature, and the second is the present status. It is difficult to grasp the exact status of the target setting, making it difficult to secure the suitability of target setting and to understand the actual state of execution. It's easy to understand that it's also a constraint on doing C and A. In short, it is because there is no visualization.

Toyota starting from C for visualization

In general, in order to start 'something', it is necessary to clarify the 'something' first, and it is easy to assume that starting with the specific action plan of the task, P, is very natural. However, no matter how good a plan is, unless the goal setting accurately reflects the situation at that time (the current state), the plan quickly loses its legitimacy.

It is true that Korea wins a lot of gold medals in taekwondo or archery, but it is the same reason that the goal of winning gold medals in Olympic Taekwondo or archery sports just because I am a Korean cannot be justified immediately.

So what really matters when running the work cycle?

The actual work process that everyone who works through is to first reflect on the past, clearly check the current state, and then thoroughly extract the problem and then establish a new improvement plan or work plan.

The goal of winning a medal at the next Olympics is realistic if I have the ability to rank first in the national competition. However, if you haven't exercised once, you have to set a goal of earning medals from a long-term perspective, starting from a lap of the town and five or ten years later. A typical example of a plan to be made without reflection or grasp of the phenomenon is the school vacation schedule. The actual cycle becomes messy if there is no clear awareness of the plan's legitimacy and phenomenon. There is no failure without reason. It is true that such a gap exists in the company's goals and vision.

So, in Toyota, I work with the CAPD cycle, not the PDCA.

In other words, Toyota starts with C, which corresponds to the identification of the phenomenon. Check

The word is deep in meaning. There are two kinds of things we often refer to as problems in business. These are 'the problem of recovery' and 'the problem of improvement'.

The problem of recovery is also called an occurrence type problem, and can be solved by maintenance and compliance with standards. It is about the existence of a principle, standard, or standard that must be followed, and how much of that principle, standard, or standard is followed. That is, there is no principle or standard, or it refers to a problem caused by not complying with it. It can be said to be a relatively low level problem.

On the other hand, the problem of improvement is also referred to as a set-up problem, and it refers to a problem that can be solved by setting a desired state in the future as a goal and overcoming the difference between the goal and the phenomenon. Growing companies means they are solving this problem of improvement.

To put it simply from the conclusion, the more problems of recovery, the more messed up the PDCA for problems of improvement becomes. The less skillful the more difficult it is to achieve the goal. However, the improvement and innovation activities that most companies promote are something that Toyota and GE have learned, but the idea that 'we need to squeeze a dry towel' or set a high 'Stretch Goal' is a very good goal. In most cases, a plan is established. But Peter Drucker's statement, "Efforts to deliver what is poorly designed, is the greatest waste," is the result of observations about such companies, a series of failures.

If you want to succeed in change, if you want to sustain it, it's very important to get a good understanding of where you are. The starting line is to "check" what is the problem of recovery that we are missing in order to jump further and higher, and how well we currently have.

In the meantime, the actions for "maintenance" and "compliance" of the standard class, which correspond to the problem of recovery discovered, is, without thinking, "Act!".

After solidifying the foundation, you can plan according to the desired future (Plan) and do it according to the plan (Do).

In that way, it can be understood that the most important activity is Check, and the accuracy of the C determines the relevance and achievement of the entire activity. This is why Toyota pursues 'visibility' in all departments and activities. The essence of visual management is not that it solves something in itself, but that it reveals the image as it is, like a good mirror.

Next, let's take a closer look at how Toyota Group and Lean Company visualize their work.

Toyota focuses on problem solving with abnormal response management

The explanations for various terms continue to appear because they must have a clear understanding of the terms before they can be executed properly. In particular, many terms used in the Toyota method, which are famous for "the study of practice," are contrary to existing common sense or have more essential meanings, so it is important to understand them well.

As mentioned earlier, there are upper and lower control limits, and the distribution within them is called normal, and the state outside the limit is called abnormality or problem. We call it "improvement" to return to a normal state by taking action on more (problem) or to raise the level of management to the next level.

Therefore, it can be seen that the prerequisite is to know whether the current state is normal or not before improvement. So-called 'visibility' is the easiest and most accurate means of knowing whether there is normality or abnormality. In addition, to explain their management responding only to the ideals, Toyota calls the management of other companies "normal management" and their management as "abnormal response management."

Normal management refers to management that must constantly check whether it is normal or not. Most of the manager's work is invested in the verification or monitoring, and when a problem occurs, it is not a recurrence prevention, but an ad-hoc measure. This refers to a type of management in which the problem recurs due to the same cause. Dare to say, many companies fall into this, except for a few companies known as Toyota and Lean Company.

On the other hand, abnormality response management secures a high level of 'visibility', so the normal is not managed. In principle, by putting effort into the countermeasures to prevent recurrence, rather than temporary measures by investing labor only when an abnormality occurs, that is, when a problem occurs, in principle, 'to prevent the problem from recurring again due to the same cause', or even at all. It means removing the management itself by devoting time to 'prevention' by eliminating the cause of such problems.

Visualization and abnormality response management will be covered in more detail in Part 2, so this is the end here.

As described above, in Part 1, mainly the perception and philosophy of Toyotism's work

Why can we solve the problems of the present times? The distinct difference

We focused on what is the advantage.

Now, in more detail, I would like to understand how to implement Toyotism by looking at the differentiated way of Toyota Motor Company and its members working. By explaining the activities carried out by Toyota Motor Company as a basis as possible, I will try to overcome the barrier of perception that the industry is different, the work is different, or the personality is different. Because acknowledging differences is for ultimate understanding, not to fix and maintain them.

PART 2.

Toyotism, the way of working is different

In Part 2, I will explain the characteristics of the organization's operation as a means of achieving goals and goals from the perspective of 'how Toyota and Lean Companies are doing their jobs'.

I hope that it will be helpful in the 'selective perception' of the system's meaning and methodology for realizing 'work within the organization' that no matter who does the job, the same result must be achieved repeatedly.

When it comes to benchmarking and introducing other companies' ideas and methodologies into their own companies, they always face a dilemma of "application" and "adaptation".

There is always a trade off relationship between the scientific factor (rational factor) in the application process and the cultural factor (irrational factor) in the adaptation process. In this part, I tried to reveal the scientific element of Toyotism, that is, the rational element as much as possible. However, in order to transfer it to the readers' corporate, organization, and personal life, friction with existing thoughts and cultures must arise. Therefore, I hope that through wise action on this, we will be able to lay the foundation for building each company's and each's competitiveness.

Chapter 7.

Toyotism-based ways of working are Agile and Lean

Frederic Laloux, who dealt with a new management paradigm, in his book 《Reinventing Organizations》, represents a paradigm of how the shape of an organization has changed and symbolizes 'color'. Well explained through.

Excluding civilization critics, the tendency to view human history as developmental history is probably a general view. However, perspectives on what is the underlying driver of such development may be different. Max Weber and Adam Smith refer to modern capitalism as 'individual selfishness is the power that motivates all progress'. Since its definition, it is true that the idea that selfish behavior leads to social good has been dominated.

However, not only analyzing the birth and dynamics of capitalism as short as 230 years, but from the perspective of 'Big History' from the origin of mankind to the present, the driving force for the development of human history that the author finds and asserts is selfishness or It is not competition, but collaboration. In fact, humans are the first and second are wolves among the existences that have the widest distribution on the planet and survive in any environment, and the greatest characteristic of the two in common is the beings who cooperate, and collaboration is the 'human victory'. Laloux says it is the cause of this.

In this book, he deals with the history of human collaboration. It shows how the paradigm of new collaboration methods and organizational culture has evolved over time and vertically. And it is believed that such a paradigm has survived horizontally up to the present, and is clarifying the case.

He gave each symbolic color to the paradigm or collaboration method of each period. It will also be meaningful to enjoy a walk through history while looking at what kind of path we have taken. Because at the end of the walk, you can meet Toyotism and Lean Company.

Paradigm change according to the change of collaboration method

Red, the authoritative governing society of the powerful Absolute

The first is the oldest paradigm, expressed in red. In an analogy, it is similar to ' a swarm of wolves '. It is the oldest organizational structure that has emerged since the primitive tribal society, and has been mainstream for millions of years. The key characteristic is that he has a powerful boss, the enemies outside fear him and the crowd inside obey him.

Such an organization is advantageous to chaos and turbulence. This is because there is no such thing as a powerful boss to guarantee the survival of the group. The core competitiveness of this organizational culture is authoritative governance. When the boss decides the direction, the crowd follows. In order to achieve the organization's common goals, division of labor begins, and specialized fields are created to promote the interests of the entire group. Even today, you can see organizations moving in this red paradigm, for example, mafia, gangsters, and pirates. These organizations are inherently short of sight. This is because survival is the urgent priority.

Yellow, strict class system and rank order society

Next is the yellow organization. Displayed when an unstable power structure based on fear governance cannot achieve long-term success. It can be likened to an "army". The class system associated with status will develop. Examples are the Roman Army and the Catholic Parish. It can be seen that it is an attempt to carry out long-term goals, not just physical strength, with reliable leadership based on class system.

The characteristic of such a yellow organization is "order and stability" through a strict class system. Seniors exercise powerful authority over their subordinates. Core competitiveness can be the title and digits of a powerful administrative "procedure" and various formulas in its rank order that adhere to long-term success. Examples of yellow perspectives that still exist today include public schools, governments and churches.

Orange, a performance-oriented society represented by reason and rationality

The next step, orange, appeared because the rigid yellow

organization failed to meet the new era. The orange symbol for organization is 'machine'. It is a representative symbol that appeared in the era of reason and rationality. Together with the American and French revolutions, it was a time when individual abilities became important. It was also around the time when they were starting to gain opportunities to participate in competition regardless of class. The dawn of the industrial revolution and capitalism that are familiar to us has finally dawned.

The main characteristics of the orange organization are "competition" inside and outside the organization, "pursuing profit maximization", and "goal-oriented management style". When a superior sets a strategy, a subordinate is given limited freedom to carry out the strategy. The core competitiveness of the orange organization can be represented by 'innovation', 'responsibility' for achieving set goals, and 'performanceism' that can be promoted according to competences such as intelligence and creativity. It is also the mainstream organizational culture paradigm of today. Almost all companies and organizations fall into this. Perhaps the company or organization of the readers reading this book is likely to belong to it.

The reason the orange organization hits its limits is when the salary increase is less effective. This is when employees start to feel that they are just small parts of the machine. According to a 2013 survey, US workers' commitment to work is only 30%, which is the limit of orange organizations. Provoking low-level needs (salary, welfare, etc.) is a common problem for companies that are no longer able to exert their power and lack of stimulation to high-level needs (a sense of belonging, recognition, etc.).

Green, a society that values participation and balance

The next step, green, naturally emerges as more people start looking for meaning in the workplace. Green organization can be compared to "family". The main values of a green organization are 'customer satisfaction', 'decision making based on shared values', and 'high participation of all members'.

Core competitiveness includes a "stakeholder balance" that encompasses the needs of all stakeholders, including customers, employees, and shareholders, as well as a tendency to value "culture" over strategy and "authorization" regardless of class. As an example of a green organization, the authors take Southwest Airlines, Ben & Jerry's, which are the attributes of agile and lean that also share the same characteristics. Frederic Laloux said that green organizations reach their limits when decisions are slowed down due to inability to form consensus. The class system that remains in the organization is in conflict with those who want greater autonomy, and I think he's seen a typical Japanese company, not Toyota Motor Company. However, as mentioned earlier, Japanese companies and Toyota are showing quite different appearances, and they are actually taking different paths. Lalu talks about Agile and Lean at this stage, but I think readers will probably discover more characteristics of Toyota and Toyota in the next stage.

Turquoise, an organic organization with integrity and autonomy

The next level of turquoise emerges as organizations discover how to work effectively without hierarchies. The symbol representing the turquoise tissue is 'life, organism'.

The main characteristic of the turquoise organization is that the more it is broken, the stronger it is (anti-fragile). When faced with a crisis, the horizontal organizational structure and roles interlock and change to become a stronger organization. It changes in line with evolving goals and visions and changes in line with the values shared by employees, which is made possible through a "advice process," in which everyone shares all decision-making powers. Anyone can make a decision as long as they accept the feedback from those who will be affected by the decision.

The core competence of the turquoise organization is expressed as 'wholeness'. Employees can fully reveal their individuality, such as their spirituality, intelligence, and creativity. Even if they show themselves as they are, they are not evaluated psychologically. Another core competency is 'autonomy'. He explains that most turquoise organizations don't have managers, they just have an evolving mission. This means that the organization's mission is not subordinated to a specific individual, but evolves and changes as people enter and leave, and as the organization learns to make a greater impact. In addition to this explanation, he includes outdoor apparel company Patagonia as an example of a turquoise organization, Morning Star, which accounts for 40% of the US tomato product market, and Buurtzorg, a home care non-profit organization consisting of 7,000 people.

Toyotism represented by Agile and Lean

From this perspective, it would be a good order to start with the reality that most companies and organizations are in the orange domain, and then understand the trend toward green or turquoise.

The higher levels of orange, Agile and Lean, have their roots in the green paradigm. Agile and Lean are often poorly introduced into organizations because leadership stays at the orange organizational level. To those who have an orange organizational perspective, Agile and Lean are just means of increasing productivity, efficiency and profits. However, it is pointed out that without the application of the 'culture' that green organizations value, if they adopt Lean, only elements such as orange innovation, responsibility, and performanceism remain, and they are buried in the values of the orange organization such as top-down management methods and profit maximization. . It cannot but be an excellent point.

Finally, he emphasizes that he does not claim that one color is necessarily better than another. Each paradigm can have its own values and strengths depending on each perspective or the maturity of each company or organization. It also means that it can depend on the members of the company and business units and the actual goals. However, it should not be understood as saying that it is okay to stay with children forever. It would be a good idea to use it as a compass to understand the stages of growth and confirm the direction to go.

just as expected! According to the data he analyzed, the colored organizational culture that appeared later can effectively handle tasks with high complexity and interconnection. But this isn't necessary for every situation, and it's not just green and turquoise organizations. Depending on the color, the definition of success is different, and although it is a natural story, the organization of the new color contains the organizational advantages of the old color. He describes this as a Russian doll, matryoshka, in which dolls of the same shape are kept inside. If you're someone with a turquoise perspective, show that you can and should continue to apply the benefits of orange and yellow tissue along with turquoise, depending on the nature of your organization.

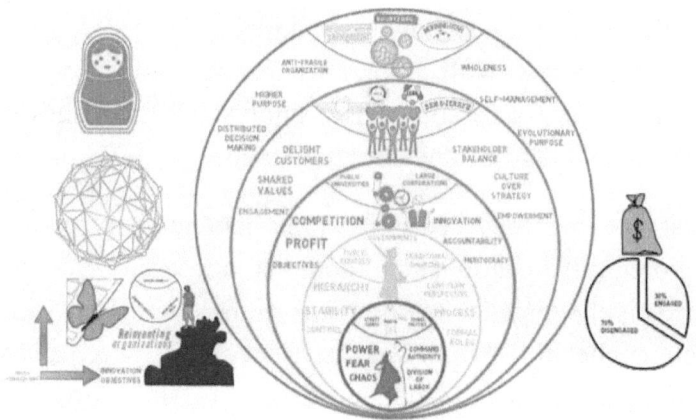

Structure and understanding of the paradigm of each era (©www.awperformances.com)

This also makes us understand why many organizations struggle in applying the Toyota method when looking at the paradigm of Toyotaism, symbolized by Agile and Lean, in terms of organizational culture. Not only that, it makes you realize how important culture is to organizational change.

The figure below shows the Toyota method. As a representative of sustainable companies, I would like to mention Toyota more than any other company, and the reason is shown in the figure. Looking at the picture, it can be seen that there are two main reasons why Toyota Motor Company has continued its 80-year history. One is

'Continuous Improvement', and the other is 'Respect for People'.

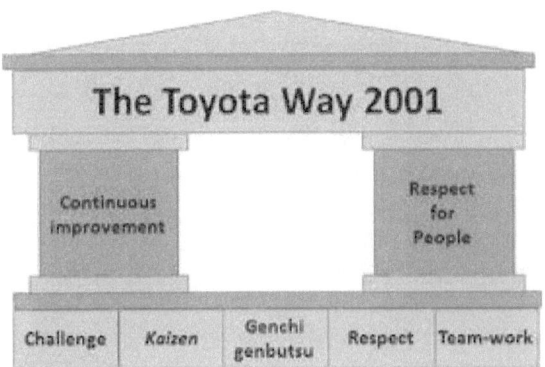

Toyota Way

The most important thing for a company that has continued for 80 years is not repeating what it did yesterday today, but constantly changing it and pursuing change, and such change is not only the company itself, but also the suppliers that exist in the entire supply chain management (SCM). Toyota knows better than anyone else and has been practicing that it is possible through respect for the company, its customers, its stakeholders and people. Few companies emphasized 'customer satisfaction' as early as Toyota's, and for the first time, a company that balances with the company and supplies most parts for customer satisfaction is called a 'partner company' rather than a 'subcontractor'. It reveals the philosophy of respect.

Now, by understanding the culture that supports Toyota's way of working and the way it works, we are more resistant to crises through a culture of 'respect for people' and 'continuous improvement', which is the core of Toyotism. Let's look at what can be an organization.

Chapter 8.

Toyotism, working systematically

System is an organism

Those at the top of the business process, such as development and design, correspond to the creation of ideal information. The job of the manufacturing sector is literally responsible for the transcription of ideal information. And the sales organization and its members are playing the role of distributing the ideal information to the outside.

Simplifying the flow of business activities, the manufacturing industry will be a continuous flow of development-production-sales, and the service industry will be a continuous flow of development-sales-performance. Everyone acknowledges that in this matter, the same results must be repeatedly derived without damaging the ideal information, no matter who does it. So, the company makes the following requests to all members.

"Work systematically!"

If so, we must first ask this question.

"What is a system?"

First, the dictionary definition of the system is as follows.

System

noun

1. 1.

Systematic method, organization, or institution

Purified words are 'organization', 'system', 'method'

"Efficient management"

2. 2.

computer

Organic combination of central processing unit, storage unit, input/output unit, communication line, etc.

For a more in-depth understanding, let's look at the definition of systems in systems theory organized by economist Kenneth Boulding in the 1950s.

"A system can be defined as a combination of elements in which one or more components are functionally related to each other in order to achieve a predetermined common purpose or goal. That is, it is a set of interrelated parts that make up the whole. In other words, a system refers to a set of interacting parts designed for a specific purpose as an assembly in which several independent constituent factors have their own functions and are organically combined with each other to achieve an overall goal. In other words, it refers to an organism in which two or more objects are united to perform a specific purpose with a logical relationship between the objects."

If we summarize the definition of Boulding above in a word, we can see that it is 'system=organism'. In fact, the word "organism" seems to be a good use of the nuances in the sense of an organization that is organically composed and has life functions like living things, rather than the words generally used when understanding a system.

However, in nature no organism is born with a purpose or goal. The same goes for people. No one is born with a goal. However, a group of people, especially in the form of a company, always has a purpose and a goal. Rather, a company is a group of people who come together to achieve those goals and goals.

If so, the company should already be a 'system as an organism that fulfills a specific purpose' in the system theory itself. This is because, as seen in the definition of a system, 'a system is a combination and an aggregate of elements in which one or more components are mutually functionally related to achieve a predetermined common purpose or goal'.

Still, why do we cry out to work systematically when we open our eyes?

What does it mean to work systematically?

In order to resolve this disparity, we must properly understand 'what is working systematically'.

Since 'system = an organism with a goal and purpose',

working systematically can be understood as having to do work that shares the same characteristics as an organism. If the system theory was born for an integrated understanding of science, we need to understand the characteristics of organisms, that is, living things in order to understand systems.

The characteristics of living things that are generally distinguished from non-living things are said to have three abilities: self-proliferation, energy conversion, and homeostasis. We can extract the concept of systemic work, that is, organic work.

So the definition of a system that I always talk about when I speak is as follows.

"A system is a structure where stable inputs, the same results, and repeated results."

Organisms, organisms, and systems multiply themselves through energy conversion (the ability to convert inputs into outputs), and have the ability to maintain homeostasis to achieve the same results over and over again.

In these simple words, we can understand what it means to work systematically. That is, you just have to work by creating a 'structure with a stable input, the same result, and repetitive appearance'. This is literally a principle of science.

At what degree does the water boil? If only the prerequisites of pure water (distilled water) and 1 atmosphere (stable input) are met, the result of boiling at 100 degrees (same result) can be obtained by elementary school students, university professors, or factory workers (repeatedly).

After all, management or management, and furthermore, what we do is to understand that it is an act to repeatedly obtain the same result (translation of the ideal information) with a stable input (media or person) including abnormal information. It is often said that things that cannot be measured cannot be managed or managed, but what we do is the science of confirming causal relationships through measurements. Or it should be such a science.

Therefore, while the system itself is defined as an organism to achieve goals and goals, the slogan to work systematically in many organizations exists because we do not know the correct definition of working systemically and how to implement it.

On the other hand, it can be said that the people working at Toyota Motor, which I used as the main subject matter in this book, always have a "system" in mind when it comes to the way they work. The system at this time does not mean computerization. However, it is also not to say that computerization should be excluded in today's development of Information Communication Technology (ICT). If so, what elements are Toyota's people using to create a structure that repeatedly produces the same results with this system, stable inputs?

Four elements to build a system

In order to build a system, it is necessary to remember the following four elements.

① Standard or rule

② Normal check tool

③ abnormality notification tool

④ Manager

First, in order to work systematically, the standards and rules for the work must be clearly defined. Different people produce different results because different people work differently. As mentioned earlier, you cannot manage or manage anything that cannot be measured. To do this, it is necessary to grasp the object in a measurable and quantitative manner, and in order to measure something, a measurement standard, that is, a measure, is necessary. This is why there must be clear standards and rules for all tasks.

Second, the normal check tool refers to a tool that can check whether the given standards and rules are well followed in the field. Since everyone is rational, they choose to do what they can and don't do if there are things they can't do. Therefore, a rule that cannot be verified results in the same situation as there are no rules. That is why it is said that the more efficient and reliable the organization is, the more the organization has a culture that the boss must confirm. However, the larger the organization, the more difficult it is for the boss to check everything one by one, so more and more of these normal check tools need to be put into the system. This has a very deep relationship with the need to give rules or standards that can be followed. How to check whether the rule can be followed or not is surprisingly simple. You can do it yourself. So, the definition of the role of the leader in Toyota is as follows.

"Try it, show it to him, and let him do it."

Try it yourself, give your subordinates the standards and rules that you can do, that you can keep, but take the means to make sure that it is normal. As many of you may have noticed, this is where 'visualization' plays an important role. Whether it is a factory or an office, Toyota judges whether it is normal through a progress control board, which is just one example.

Third, it is an abnormality notification tool, which can be said to be a tool that informs when a situation out of standards or rules occurs. The easiest way is to create a tool that can notify you with light and sound when an abnormality occurs. Representative examples are the Andon (electronic board, status board) used in Toyota's field, and the task board, a visual management tool used in the office sector. Toyota's autonomation is the origin of the structure in which the facilities used in the factory make a sound and automatically stop when an abnormality occurs. It means that we have to expand this to the area where people work.

Lastly, the person in charge is the person who is responsible for restoring the abnormality to normal. Just as everyone's responsibility is nobody's responsibility, one criterion, rule, always needs someone to take responsibility for the results. Responsibility here refers to the returning of the ideal to normal and improvement activities to achieve the goal by bridging the gap between the present and the goal. In the office sector, if there is a lot of transfer of powers and responsibilities, the practitioner may be in charge. However, in the manufacturing industry or service industry, the responsible person at this time is the supervisor or manager. This is because field employees in the manufacturing industry or frontline employees in the service industry are usually required to act according to a given work standard or manual. Of course, it is generally encouraged to offer suggestions for better results or to act on surprise services.

Start of Toyota-style system work, automation

When I go to Toyota Motor Company training in Nagoya, Japan, there are places I always visit. It is the Industrial Technology Memorial Hall. It is a memorial hall that 13 companies of Toyota Group invested in to understand the development of industrial technology through textile machinery and automobiles.

Toyota Motor Vehicle Industrial Technology Museum in Nagoya

The Toyota Group's roots are in textile machines called Toyota automatic looms, and what made the Toyota Group today is also the fruit of the automobile industry. However, there is another reason for exhibiting textile machinery and automobiles here. This is because the most core concepts of the Toyota Production System (TPS), Autonomation and JIT (Just in Time) were acquired in the process of developing the textile machinery and automobile industries, respectively.

Automation means that when an abnormality or defect

occurs, a machine or facility detects it by itself and stops it. Its history is as follows.

In 1896, Sakichi Toyota invents the automatic loom. As is well known, since the Industrial Revolution centered on the textile industry in the UK, automatic weaving machines already existed in the world. However, since the loom continued to operate even when the thread was broken or the lower thread (weft) was exhausted, female workers had to be placed in front of the loom one by one to take action. In general, this state is called 'One man, one machine'. However, Sakichi invented a loom that could detect and stop when the thread was cut or the lower thread was used up. In other words, because it moves with the human autonomic nerve, it is called autonomation. As a result, there is no need for surveillance, so a single female worker can take charge of multiple looms. That is why the Japanese textile industry, which was initially only a tenth of the productivity of the UK, was able to overcome the 10-fold difference in productivity and surpass the UK's textile industry. In summary, the first meaning of autonomation can be called an 'auto stop' function.

In this way, we faced the problem of how to apply the concept that was initially applied to facilities to a manual line where humans work, and the answer is the 'Line Stop' system that can be easily seen on the assembly line of

Toyota Motors. In the manual line, people work, so the authority to stop the line is given to the worker who is best aware of the abnormality or defect. It is also a scene rarely seen in other companies. However, compared to the fact that a large number of defects occur while the decision on whether to stop or not to stop the line is delayed, Toyota's line stop system allows the line to be stopped on the spot when an abnormality or defect occurs. It makes a significant contribution to improvement. Therefore, the second meaning of autonomation can be called 'Built in Quality'. 'Line stop' is not proud of the manufacturing industry, so if you ask the essential question, whether they do 'line stop', it will be easy to understand. It means that even by stop the line, we should solve the abnormality or quality problem and pass on to the next process. 'Quality must be secured in the process. It expanded to the idea that I will never pass the defects to the next process.' That's how the image of "Toyota of quality" was created.

The four elements of the system and automation

In the course of explaining Toyota's automation, I am going to further explain four elements of the system. Take a look at the following picture.

The loom shown in the photo is an automatic loom developed by Sakichi. The concept of autonomation was applied, and before this loom was developed, it was just an automatic loom.

Automatic loom developed by Toyota Sakichi

As mentioned earlier, since the existing automatic loom only moved continuously, one female worker was deployed per machine, and if the thread was exhausted or the thread was cut, it was quickly recognized and the machine was stopped and no action was taken. It didn't work. The problem was solved by Sakichi Toyota, and the concept was called Autonomation in contrast to Automation.

Sakichi's loom basically has the function of detecting and stopping the machine itself when the thread runs out or when the thread is cut. That way, the surveillance work of female workers was eliminated. Let's look at how the loom detects a broken thread.

Automatic stop device simulator when thread is cut

The simulator in the photo has 4 threads installed to aid understanding. And the red thread breaks. When the thread does not break, the loom moves normally, and when the thread breaks, the machine detects it and stops it. When you press the switch on the simulator, the loom starts to move by itself. After going back and forth several times, if the red thread in the picture is squeezed downwards and cuts, the loom stops soon.

Substituting the four elements of the system into this loom, the standard and rule is 'stop when the thread is broken'. If so, there is also a tool for checking the normal to detect that the thread is not broken, and a tool to notify the abnormality when the thread is broken. When the abnormality notification tool notifies of abnormality, the machine itself takes on the role of the person in charge or the manager and finally stops the operation. Therefore, system construction can be achieved simply by securing a normal check tool and a tool for notifying abnormalities. That's why Sakichi built a system by creating a normal check tool and a tool to communicate abnormalities.

Let's look at the picture again. If you look closely, you will notice that there is a thin metal rod hanging on each slope. It is easy to guess that if the red thread breaks, the metal rod that has lost tension will fall down. It becomes a tool to inform the ideal and stops the loom.

abnormality notification tool   normal check tool

The normal check tool is the hacksaw-like shaft on the right. Check the normality by reciprocating exactly about 6 centimeters back and forth. Then, when the red thread breaks, the thin metal rod on the left side of the thread falls down, narrowing the movement distance of the hacksaw-like shaft. At that moment, the metal rod serves as a abnormality notification tool. Soon the loom stops. Through this simulator, we can easily understand the four elements of the system by visually checking them.

The improvement cases of Toyota Motor Company and its partners are all the result of efforts to build the four elements of this system on their site. This is the most important concept to understand and implement Toyotism, so I want to emphasize that it is necessary to remember it.

It can be said that the system was finally established when the above four elements (in fact, in most cases, the normality check tool and the abnormality notification tool often achieve their purpose at the same time). And when you do that, you can say that you work systematically.

As a result, it can be seen that the center of work can shift to management responding only to abnormalities instead of naturally managing normality in this way. In the field, the method of managing abnormalities is called 'changing point management,' and it is active on two axes: prevention in advance and prevention of recurrence of unexpected problems.

In Toyota, just like visualizing the manufacturing line that makes things, efforts to reveal problems, find the cause of the problem, and resolve it through the visualization of the manufacturing line (office division) that creates information continues.

Chapter 9.

Visualization determines the success or failure of a system

A lot of things can be solved just by revealing a problem

You are all familiar with Andersen's short story, The Naked King. The contents are as follows.

There was a king who was incompetent and only liked clothes. One day, two tailors appeared in front of the king, claiming to know how to make the best clothes in the world from the most beautiful fabrics in the world. The king rejoices and gives them a large sum of money to make them fancy clothes. The two tailors, ordered by the king, say, "The fabric is a fabric that is invisible to a foolish idiot."

After that, the king was suspicious of the tailors and sent a servant to check the completeness of the clothes. The officers who went to spy on the tailor could not see the clothes clearly, and they were just pretending to make clothes in the air. However, the servant lied to the king that the clothes were being made for fear that he would appear to be a fool, and other servants dispatched afterwards lied that they could see the clothes for the same reason. Finally, one day, the tailors present the clothes to the king, saying they are finished.

But the king also can't see the clothes! However, since the officials have said that they can see the clothes, the king also praises them as beautiful clothes, fearing that people will point to him as an idiot if he say he cannot see them. And the king wears the clothes that the tailors put on. Of course, the tailors only pretended to dress, and the king also pretended to be dressed.

The king wears clothes and goes out on the street. In fact, the clothes were not visible in the eyes of everyone, including people and servants on the street, but they couldn't say anything because they didn't want to be fools. But a little boy shouted, "Your Majesty the king is naked!", and finally everyone and the king realize that he is not wrong, but that he really has no clothes. However, the king ignores it because of his face and continues on his way.

The essence of this story is not that the king is a fool full of vanity, but that all adults are fools except for one child who knows and laughs. And surprisingly, the "solution" to this situation was the child's laughter and bomb declaration. With just one laughter, all adults awakened to their own shame.

It shows in an easy-to-understand way how lies are made, expanded and reproduced, and finally becomes the dominant "natural" of society or organization. It also shows that knowing the truth is not difficult, but it is also difficult to tell the truth. Not because we don't know, but because we don't like to accept "discomfort," or because we are afraid of "disadvantage," we cannot speak or act. Andersen shows how fragile the base of lies is and how simple problems can be solved by very easily 'revealing the facts' by introducing an innocent child at the end.

First, let's look at the process of generating falsehood and the process of expanding reproduction.

In the story, a veteran servant who went to check the production situation of clothes after receiving the first order of the king, rubbed his eyes again and again and looked through the empty loom, but he lied for fear of being seen as a fool. Subsequently, the next servant and even the king participate in the process of expanding and reproducing falsehood, and the falsehood now gains its own power and becomes more and more justified and amplified, finally taking the "place of fact". Really everyone takes it for granted.

This is exactly the same for companies. It shows well the phenomena that are still frequently occurring among managers, managers, and employees. Anyone who denies the lie within the organization is stigmatized as a mad deviant. There was something for everyone to keep or hide with a tremendous weight. If it is not revealed, it goes through the process of praising the boss and approving his loyalty, and surprisingly, it acts as a safety plate to preserve me in reverse.

In the conviction created by that misinformation and behavior, wages or managers make false judgments. It is 'going to the street'. In the end, however, the judgment ends with a tragedy that reveals that the judgment was wrong and foolish due to the disclosure of the facts of only one person (the child who told the truth in the story).

This is where we can see the importance and power of 'visualization'. This is why Toyota puts so much emphasis on visualization that many problems can be solved by itself just by revealing the 'facts.' Man is not perfect. So, there is a 'possibility' that can make mistakes, weaken before power, and become ugly or vicious for one's own success. On the other hand, it is also the existence of 'possibility' that everyone can find their place just by confronting the truth once. Management is investing in that 'possibility'.

It is a management problem, not a person, so a system is needed.

Visualization or visible management is to organize the process of work in all spaces where work is done into easy-to-manage units, and to make it possible to grasp the actual situation at a glance. Through this visualization, anyone can know the subject matter of the problem, and because the problem is revealed, it will be possible to make improvement, management innovation, and strategic decisions "rightly" as soon as possible. 'Quick' reveals speed, that is, JIT thought. 'Properly' reveals the idea of quality, that is, automation. It is Visualization that makes automation and JIT, the two main axes of Toyotaism, not only a concept or an idea, but a concrete reality.

The management skills for downstream processes working at the enterprise level of ideal information have reached a fairly high level. However, it is true that the upstream process, which is the stage of creating ideal information, so-called management skills for office workers, is not very high. The main reason is that it is not possible to see if the employees are working or not. Therefore, in order to realize a high level of management, the following six elements must be equipped.

① Visualization of work

② Improvement (exclusion or removal of non-value work and non-value-added work)

③ Creating the flow of work (pursuit of JIT, system synchronization)

④ 3 Reals (see the real thing in the real field and understand the real phenomenon. There is an answer in the field)

⑤ polyfunctionalization of human resources (motivation through expansion of work)

⑥ Standardization (sharing judgment criteria)

These six are also processes to increase work productivity.

First reveal the work. Then you will see what you must do and what you don't need to do. You can agree to get rid of things you don't have to do naturally (non-value work, non-value added work). When we learn that the overall lead time is increasing due to congestion between individuals and between individuals and between departments and between departments, we come to the conclusion that each must keep the flow of work in a consistent manner. Not only is it easy to understand that one person must have a variety of work abilities in order to fill in excesses and shortages, and this is the basis for nurturing human resources, and it is also a means of strong motivation. And the results thus obtained are shared by everyone as a standard.

The greatest effect of visualization is that it can lead to consciousness reform of the entire organization. In fact, unlike the work of machines or robots, it is true that human work has large variations and fluctuations in its performance. If we look at it only in terms of individual differences, in the end the responsibility lies with the individual, and only dismissal will be the answer. But if you look at it as a management problem, not a human problem, you can see that a system is needed here as well. And the success or failure of a system depends on visualization.

The important thing here is that it is 'Visualization', not 'surveillance'. By making them realize the existence of a problem through visualization, it is intended to promote a cycle of growth of thinking, speaking, acting, and reflecting. We are never trying to create people who are passive and respond only to instructions by monitoring every step of the way, and they shouldn't. This is of great importance in that the difference in human perspective determines the overall direction of system operation.

It should be understood that visualization is a philosophy and methodology that transforms the management of others into self-management.

Through visualization activities, companies can generally improve performance and improve the quality of relationships within the organization. It is natural that an organization that understands the mission, vision, strategy, and purpose and can link it with functional competencies has high performance. Therefore, a culture of success will build on its own if an organization allows its employees to decide and execute for themselves what they need, how to do it, and by when. In addition, visualization makes us aware of the company's purpose to increase customer satisfaction by providing what customers really need and want, when they want, and as much as they want. Furthermore, by focusing on performance thoroughly, it improves productivity and eliminates wasted elements, thereby creating a more efficient culture of execution.

The improvement of employee satisfaction and the quality of relationships within the organization through visualization is of greater importance in terms of sustainable management. Everyone wants to join a winning team. Even more or less onlooked people change their attitudes toward work and organization when someone is eager to innovate, seeing the positive effects of the effort, and when they are involved, when they feel that their contributions are recognized by the organization. As the concentration on work increases, the satisfaction level increases. And everyone understands how to work closely with co-workers to achieve their goals, and credibility increases.

For those trying to do something, visualization acts like a video board for a baseball field. Whatever you are in, you can instantly see all of them at a glance, and help you decide what to do and how you are going. But for those who aren't trying to do something, visualization will feel like CCTV. It is not the organization that makes visualization into surveillance, but perhaps the members. This is because, unless the objective is for the manager to control everything, the antipathy for visualization is likely to be related to his or her attitude in the end.

In addition, managers should also do high-level

management in which everyone becomes a winner by enhancing execution power at the previous stage, rather than performing low-level management using visualization as a means of evaluating individual performance based on results.

Toyota, which has built this enterprise-wide visualization, is interested in how it will achieve the way it works for overall optimization. In the next chapter, we will look at how to organize an organization as a means of achieving our goals.

Chapter 10.

Apple and Google imitate Toyota's cross-functional organization

The Obeya method that brought Toyota back up

'G21'.

It is the name of a secret project that Toyota started in the early 1990s with the goal of developing a new concept car for the 21st century. The short-term goal was to develop a car with more than twice the fuel economy compared to existing vehicles.

It was Inoue, the head of the product planning department at the time, who created the momentum for the birth of this new concept car. At that time, it was a serious situation where profits were zero due to the yen phenomenon, and the financial sector was under pressure on costs. Regulations to reduce overtime were enforced across the company, and the Ministry of Technology was also told to regulate overtime. Manager Inoue said, "Even if you are trying to do something new, 'use the existing one. Don't make new attempts that cost money. It was a time when I was only performing the VE unilateral task of reducing the cost somehow." He thought it was natural to push VE strongly in such a situation, but it shouldn't be. Employees who thought it was pathetic to live without their dream as a technician fell into morale. At that time, the head of Inoue came up and suggested that 'in this state, it is product planning and that it is impossible to do anything and promote a new project.'

In general, when developing a new car, you use the parts that already exist, but he suggested, "Let's do a whole new design and make a whole new car." The project was officially started as the honorary chairman of Eiji Toyota actively supported this proposal.

Toyota has chosen Takeshi Uchiyamada, who has no experience in car development and design, as the technical manager for the "G21". The intention of Toyota executives who chose him, who had only accumulated experience in the field of noise and vibration, was special. In order to develop a new concept car, it was decided that a "new person" who was not immersed in the existing development system was suitable. That's how the adventure began.

And as a result, it was a success to hire him. He worked

on the project in the so-called "Obeya System (QVS, Quickening Visualization System)," that is, "a way in which all engineers who participate in G21 gather in one space to discuss in real time". Uchiyamada has created an atmosphere where people can freely discuss regardless of age and rank. When decisions can be made through impromptu discussion, the project will surely run efficiently. The period from the production of the clay model to the start of production was only 15 months. The world's first hybrid car, the Prius, was born that way. It was surprising considering that the US automakers' development period for new cars was 5-6 years at the time. The secret that Toyota was able to release hybrid cars two years earlier than its competitors was in the "Obeya method," which drove away from the existing business practices. This Obaya method, one of the sources of Toyota Motor's strengths, is now spreading all over the world and continuing its evolution. Many companies, including Ford, Volvo, GM, and Harley-Davidson, have adopted the Obaya method for the purpose of improving the quality and efficiency of product development, sales, and service. It is achieving great results by evolving according to the local circumstances of each company.

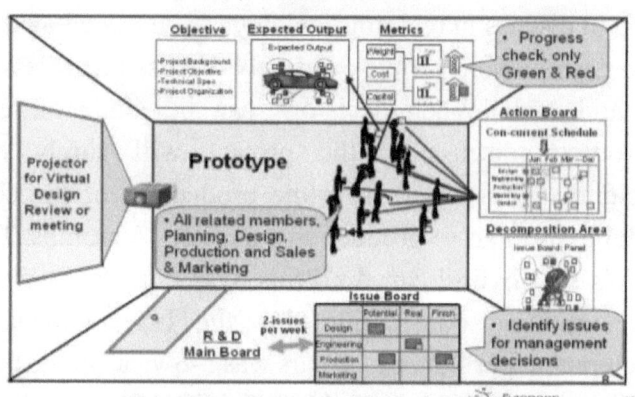

Source: Oobeya – Next Generation of Fast Product Development

Obeya method

Toyota's innovative team play, Shusa(chief engineer) system

After the financial crisis in 2008, the view that 'the pyramid-type organization is out of date in the era where speed is important' has spread. Since then, everyone has become accustomed to the mindset of 'a flat-network type organization in which all employees except the top one are equal, and each one is connected to IT and works.' Apple and Samsung, represented by Steve Jobs and Chairman Kun-hee Lee, can be said to be successful examples of such images.

A system in which all decision rights are concentrated on one person certainly does not have any aspect suitable for an era of rapid decision-making and extreme change.

On the one hand, however, it is also true that there is a structural flaw in that all employees only wait for one-saw's instructions and do not judge themselves, resulting in the inability to foster the next generation of leaders. In addition, as the organization grows, the number of places that the management cannot see increases, and because of internal competition, no one tries to see other people's circumstances, and because people are not nurtured, it is likely that the organizational power is gradually weakened. Vice Chairman Jae-yong Lee, who started to lead Samsung on behalf of Chairman Kun-hee Lee, is the result of such anxieties that 'breaking the single Samsung culture' and 'pursuing colorful Samsung' as new catch phrases.

In order to compensate for the weakness of flattening from a vertical perspective, it can be said that a 'project-type organization' from a horizontal perspective, and a 'matrix organization by product' rather than a function-specific organization.

Toyota is strong in promoting project-oriented work. When something is set, a project is created for this goal, and the task is handled by agile execution. Organizations with the letter "BR" in front of the organization name are project organizations. BR stands for Business Reform, and it refers to a "cross-functional organization" that gathers people from related departments. In Toyota, various BR organizations, large and small, are organized with mobility, and are active vertically and horizontally. While the organization on the outward organization chart is dedicated to achieving today's goals, the invisible BR organization takes on a specific theme to create the future and works intensively for a limited time. Toyota, a giant organization, is not rigid, and the secret that can lead the world in the field of hybrid cars and fuel cell vehicles is that there is an undisclosed organization called BR.

Now that there are no companies that do not operate temporary and functional organizations such as the so-called TFT (Task Force Team) or CFT (Cross Functional Team), you may laugh at these explanations, but Toyota created a cross-functional organization and lasted more than 60 years. It was in 1953 when the "shusa system" (which is now introduced by many companies, and is also referred to as the "chief engineer system") was first introduced.

From 1953, Toyota introduced the ``shusa system," which recruits and nurtures talented talents, gathers professionals in each field of expertise to create outstanding products. It is a special system that is operated in consideration of). It is operated in a way that provides full authority over all matters (development, production, sales, and service) of the product in charge to a specific person. Eiji Toyota, who served as the first president of Toyota Motor Company, said the following about shusa.

"Shusa is the president of the product, and as the president, I am the helper of shusa."

In other words, shusa is planning (product planning, product planning, sales planning, profit planning, etc.), development (industrial design, design, startup, evaluation, etc.), production and sales (equipment investment, production management, sales promotion, etc.)), and take full responsibility for the results. Since shusa's field in charge is not limited to the technical field, it is different from the general chief engineer or product manager of the development department in that respect. Since the shusa system was introduced in 1953, the name of the organization has been changed to shusa office, product planning office, development center, etc. to the present.

Surprisingly, however, this shusa only has personnel rights for his direct subordinates, and does not have a single personnel rights for project team members in departments related to planning, development, production, and sales. The only authority given to him is the 'right to persuade and adjust.'

So, shusa has no choice but to consistently explain 'why is it necessary?' and 'why can this project have a high probability of success?'

The reason why shusa is not given the right to personnel and command is because 'if shusa's proposal is valid, the other party will be convinced, and if shusa explains with all sincerity, the other party will understand.' That is why shusa builds his ability as a shusa by 'thinking of a reasonable and suggestion that will give the other person a merit' or 'an activity that enhances the persuasive power by accumulating sincere humanity and success' in order to implement his policy. If shusa's personality and achievements are recognized, it is said that even if shusa's explanations lack convincing power, there are cases where it ends with 'If shusa talks so far, it would be better to believe and follow.' On the contrary, if you don't get the credibility of an in-house or partner company, you have to withdraw from the job of shusa.

How broad is the ability required of shusa to pursue work with so much power over a single product? If you look at the "10 important mindset to vehicle shusa" left by Hasegawa, the first Carola shusa, you can estimate the range to some extent.

1) shusa must have his own tactics. People don't follow just by 'please ask'.

2) shusa should always have broad knowledge and vision. Sometimes, knowledge and insights other than specialized fields are very important. Make an effort to have 'specialty fields other than specialty fields'.

3) The shusa should make it a habit to hit the net wide. In some cases, the future is determined by 'where to start from broad view.'

4) shusa pursue omnipotence. You shouldn't give anyone the impression that you're opening your chest and looking for a hole to escape from the start.

5) shusa should not be afraid of constant repetition. You have to "reflect every day" about yourself, "continuously persuade" your boss, and "continue to seek understanding" of your partners.

6) shusa should not blame anyone else for his work. The reason for failure is not because of lack of authority, but because of lack of persuasion. Don't be angry with others over the results.

7) shusa must have confidence (belief) in herself. Do not be shaken Don't reveal it on your face even if it shakes.

8) shusa and subordinate are the same person. To rebuke, rebuke yourself.

9) shusa shouldn't be tricky. It doesn't last long with friendship, backdoor dealings, or authority.

10) The traits needed for shusa: knowledge, skill, insight, judgment (possibility), determination, measure, experience and achievements (including failure) and beliefs, not being emotional, being cold, sometimes killing oneself and being patient, concentration , Leadership, flexibility, expressiveness, persuasive power (because there is no correct answer, save your personality), aversion to greed (work for the company, not for your seat).

What if there were such a boss? What if I myself became this kind of person? This is a topic worth thinking about. In Japan, having such skills and abilities, as well as humanity and humanity that attracts people, is called 'human power'. In other words, it would be quick to understand it as 'ability + charm = human power'. From the standpoint of a company, it will not be simple to cultivate people with such human power.

Toyota's way of working, project-type work focused on horizontal linkage

The picture below shows Toyota's 'working method by project unit', which prepares for the future of the organization by nurturing human resources.

For example, when one person is being shusa, the necessary personnel are selected from each functional organization. In such a case, the human power possessed by the shusa can be an important criterion of judgment for subordinates when it comes to choosing whom to work for. Development-Production preparation-Production-Sales- When their work is terminated as a series of processes proceeds, the selected personnel return to the existing department and take charge of the task of achieving today's goals or support other projects. For example, everyone involved in a project that develops and produces a 2016 Camry Hybrid, whether he is a developer, a production engineer, a manufacturing engineer, or a salesperson, is working in the aspect that everyone must be held responsible for the product. There will be a significant difference in immersion and achievement. Relevant department members who participated in such a project will naturally have the idea of being a team, devote themselves to the success of the product in terms of overall optimization beyond departmental egoism, and will have love and pride.

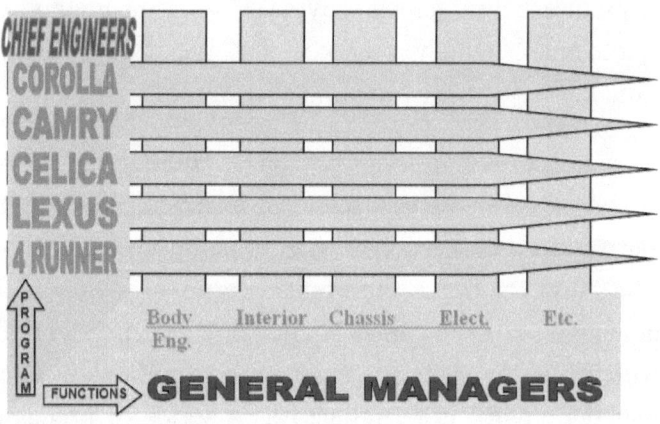

Functional crossing organization of Toyota shusa system

Similarly, in each functional organization that needs to achieve today's goals, various committees are set up to work cross-functionally with a focus on problem solving. The following figure shows the organization by function, each committee that achieves today's goal, and the organization by product of the injection system preparing for tomorrow.

As seen above, it is clear that Toyota has introduced a project-type work method early and has been implementing it for more than 60 years. Of course, just starting first doesn't guarantee you'll do well. Nevertheless, one of the reasons we can say that Toyota is good at project-type work like BR organizations is that there is an element that can be called a "network support system" as Toyota's internal corporate culture. No matter how important the project is, it is difficult to achieve the expected effect simply by gathering people who do not know each other. It cannot be accomplished with slogans alone to gather people who do not know each other well and to'find the best way through unconventional debate and controversy. Therefore, the reason why Toyota runs the project organization smoothly is that the members who already knew the other party to some extent before the construction stage and had a good feeling with each other participate. Toyota Motor Company is a large organization with 70,000 employees in Japan. It's a huge organization that can be said to be like people from other companies with different departments, but Toyota's employees know each other.

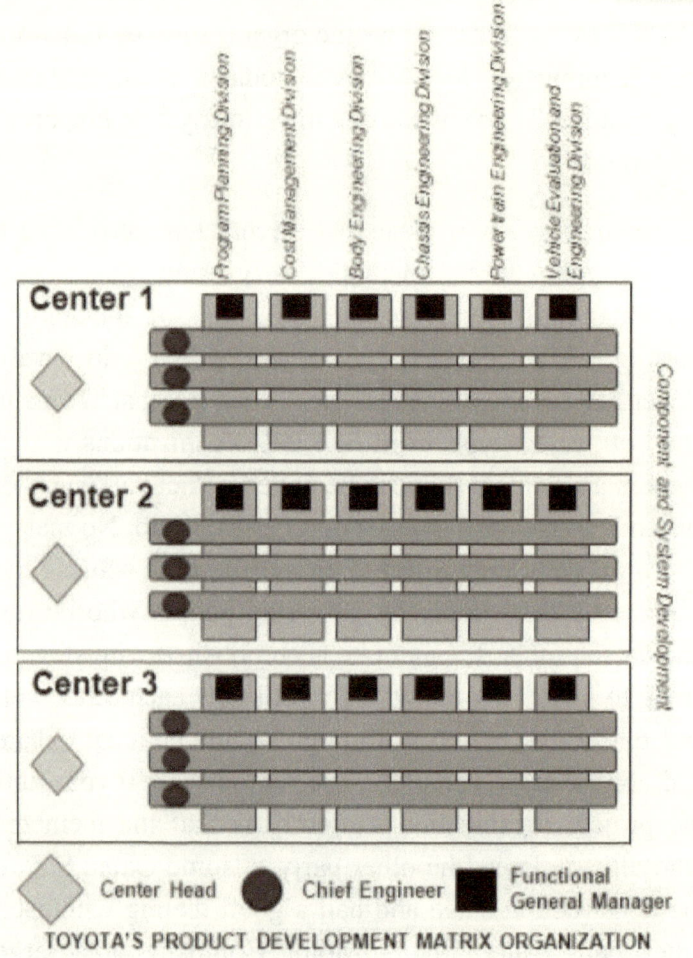

TOYOTA'S PRODUCT DEVELOPMENT MATRIX ORGANIZATION

Global Business Consulting, which I work for, is the only Korean consulting company that has its own Japanese advisors from Toyota Group, and not only Toyota Motors, but also a group of 25 advisors from Toyota Motors' partners, many of whom have known each other even during active duty. It is said that the background was based on the group's self-research group as a representative of each company and carrying out improvement activities together.

In the past, a domestic group company contacted me and conducted consulting to benchmark Toyota's personnel and labor practices. With Mr. Hiroshi Gankoji, who also published a book titled "Exports of Toyota Labor Management" while still in office, he spent a total of 4 days listening to and inquiries about Toyota's labor-management relations, the philosophy and methodology of labor management, and the wage system. I had time to do it. Toyota, which had a bitter experience through the fierce bankruptcy crisis and the great workers' struggle in 1950, was making great efforts to avoid causing such distrust between labor and management again. I remember being thrilled to hear the words that expressed such efforts in one word.

"Why did you act to make your subordinates trust the union more than you?"

It wasn't just job skills that Toyota demanded of management staff. If the person in charge of listening to the opinions of subordinates, reflecting the voices of the field, and conveying the company's values and policies does not have the necessary humanity such as consideration, charm, and respect, no matter how competent and competent, the people around him Is that this will not support you. It demands that you have so-called human power.

Labor union as an institution and system, rather than providing an opportunity to give employees a sense of achievement and self-growth in the natural daily work of people, improving the stability and quality of life for employees You're asking what you've done for these demanding things. As of 2014, the average annual employee salary of Toyota Motor Company is 7.94 million yen. It is about 80 million won in our money. The stability of life or improvement of the quality of life cannot be achieved with money alone. Rather, suffocating office workers is more of a problem such as unfairness in evaluation, a sense of accomplishment in work, a workplace atmosphere in which they cannot feel that they are growing, and relationships with bosses and colleagues. As a boss, I was amazed at the question of what kind of interest did you have in those things, what kind of conversation activities you did, what opportunities you gave them, and how did you foster them.

Toyota's horizontal linkage system benchmarked by US companies

In summary, Toyota has been operating project-type work that emphasizes lateral linkage since 1953 and in earnest since the 1960s in order to avoid information disconnection and department egoism in departmental organizations divided by function.

Unlike the temporary and functional organization to achieve the company's goals, however, it has not stopped its efforts to create a structure in which information flows, people interact and works through numerous informal groups and human relations activities that can normally have human interaction and ties.

In comparison, how many organizations are cynical about information being cut off, no communication, departmental egoism prevalent, and so there's nothing that can and shouldn't? Of course, some criticize or criticize Toyota's culture as a structure that monitors workers and keeps people vertically and horizontally.

However, this is a misunderstanding caused by a failure to properly grasp Toyota's structure and spirit. It's just a narrow perspective that compares the experiences of things you haven't been through to your own narrow experiences. Toyota's project-type work that emphasizes lateral linkage was not a system created to monitor and imprison employees working from a negative perspective. Rather, it helps employees learn to work in various fields and build a lot of networks based on a positive perspective. It is a system maintained to help people feel more fulfilled and grow more by working with different people. Otherwise, if the system had been operated for the purpose of monitoring employees, Toyota would not have been sustainable for the long 80 years. Of course, it would not have grown into a world-class company with the best performance and results.

In fact, Toyota Motor Corp. tends to see the problem as a management problem rather than to individual employees. When viewed as a management problem, not an individual problem, the manager believes that there is work to be done and that the management cycle can turn. In the name of "innovating the organization," Toyota is wary of rebuking employees such as "do it right." Instead, the manager thinks once more to give rules that can be followed, and works together to get things going. In addition, employees value so-called "organization of innovation" in order to proactively match their goals with the company's goals.

So, I set the motto of Global Business Consulting to 'organize innovation, not innovate the organization'. The implication is that it is better to work with people who are good at working with people who are good at people and those who are prospective rather than dismissing people who are bad or negative. This is because it is better not to disintegrate as individuals, but to spread the innovation virus so that everyone can gather their voices and show their skills. Of course, these thoughts were also solidified as I looked into and studied Toyota.

In fact, a company is an entity that contributes through socially meaningful work. No matter how much money a drug sales organization or a prostitution organization makes, even a large organization with a large number of people, we do not treat them as companies because their work is not socially good. Therefore, companies must do 'good customers, good sales companies, and good for society'.

However, unlike organizations such as volunteer organizations and foundations, companies are also organizations that have a mission to procure with their own resources even the resources necessary to do such 'socially meaningful work.' A foundation or an association, whether it is money or a person, already has the resources to achieve its purpose or is donated by society. However, companies must also procure resources for such activities on their own. In order to do that, a certain amount of profit is 'necessary'. Profit is not a sufficient condition, but a necessary condition. Both managers and employees need to be aware of this. However, there are still many entrepreneurs who think that the purpose of a company is to pursue profit. However, it is important to take a closer look at how many employees are getting exhausted between their own corporate ideology (mainly in the frame) and the profit-oriented reality they actually emphasize.

Here are some important principles in doing business. This means that the results of our work should be good for the company, good for customers, and good for society. It is only under this philosophy that pursuing the goal of profit is justified. One of the effective "means" for achieving goals with such justification is "organization" or "organizational system". The company's demands of 'pursuing overall optimization' or 'do not work for the position, work for the company' can become a strong and confident demand based on these premise. It is necessary to refer to Toyota's "project-type work method that emphasizes horizontal connection" as one of the efforts to strive for long-term and stable employment of employees and pursue efficiency under customer-centered values.

In fact, the first thing that paid attention to Toyota's shusa system was Americans.

In 1983, Toyota Motor Corp. and General Motors (GM) founded the merged company NUMMI (New United Motor Manufacturing Inc.), and since then many Americans have visited Toyota. The United States, which has allowed Japan to turn around in terms of manufacturing competitiveness since the 1970s, had the opportunity to see and learn the essence of Toyota. After they returned to the United States, the shusa system was delivered to Silicon Valley, and the shusa system was combined with finance to complete the ecosystem. As a representative example, it is the "iPhone" that Steve Jobs played the role of shusa as the center of development. These organizational operations and processes are organized as a "Lean Development Process" and are introduced and operated by more than 200 companies around the world.

Other companies can also become organizations optimized for the 21st century. We can make our own way. If Toyota can do that, we can do better.

In that sense, I believe that Toyota Motors and Toyotism can and should be separated at any time. As Ford Motors did not construct all of the so-called Fordism philosophy and methodology, we believe that Toyota Motors' ideas and methodology are appropriate to solve the challenges of the times of companies living in the 21st century. The reason for this is that Toyotism is only in its steps now, and it is believed that it is already spreading and developing to many companies other than Toyota Motor Company. The word to see the moon may be a subtle metaphor for the word to see the sun that illuminates the moon. Repeatedly, you have to remove Toyota from your head to see Toyotism.

Chapter 11.

Fostering human resources while solving problems

Toyota method focusing on problem solving

Work= maintenance + improvement

It is necessary to rethink the expression above. It seems that there will be less man-hour to maintain, but in fact, this is not an easy task either.

It was called an abnormality or a problem that deviated from the top. In addition, the gap between the goal and the phenomenon is also a problem. In this way, there are two forms of 'problem'. One is the 'occurrence-type problem' as the meaning of the trouble that has already occurred to maintain and the 'set-type problem' that has been artificially set in order to achieve a better desirable appearance. Then we can redefine work as:

Work = Occurrence type problem solving + Setting type

problem solving

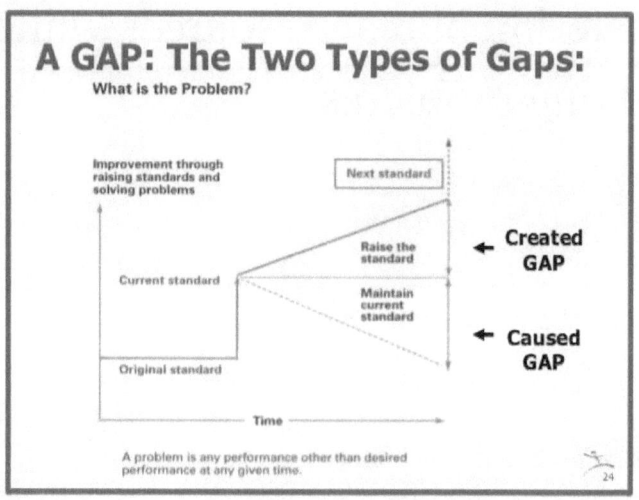

After all, what we do can be defined as a series of problem solving. There are three things Toyota puts out as a leader's condition: "problem discovery", "idea creation", and "execution". There is a saying that not knowing the problem is the biggest problem. As a joke, there is also a saying that the biggest problem of the problem child is that he has no problem consciousness itself. Toyota's corporate culture is also characterized by taking for granted the things we take for granted on a daily basis. It is most important to reveal the problem. If you don't know the problem, you can't solve it.

To solve the 'occurrence type problem', Toyota's most

commonly used technique is '5why'. What we usually call a problem is a fact and a phenomenon. However, there is another reason that caused such a phenomenon. Whether a machine breaks down or lacks communication within the organization, this is both a phenomenon and a result, not a cause. That is why Toyota clearly uses the definitions of 'problem', 'true cause', and 'task'.

First of all, 'problem' refers to a phenomenon as a perceived result. It refers to situations such as a machine stopped or sales are low. In order to grasp the true cause that caused such a phenomenon, methods such as '5why' and 'cause&effect diagram' are used to find the real cause. The real cause at this time is called 'true cause'. Since multiple causes can act on a single phenomenon, it can be said that the problem consists of numerous true causes. The target of the activities to solve the identified problems is called the 'task'. You can understand it as a problem as a task to be performed.

This thinking process is the same for setting-type problems. It is a method of finding the cause of the gap between the desired appearance and the phenomenon and performing actions on it as a task.

'Problem solving' and 'Talent development' can secure a point of contact in the part of who and what role in the organization are responsible for solving such problems. Every organization has a hierarchy. Including management, there are layers in charge of strategy and decision-making, the management layer in charge of using tactics and management to carry out such strategies, and the employee layer as the frontline performing tactical actions. Since many companies are now adopting a team system, it might be easier to understand the division into manager-team leader-team members. In this structure, we fulfill our respective roles and responsibilities (Role & Responsibility).

As is often seen, the executive organization performs tasks in order to achieve today's goals in a defined role and discipline. Nevertheless, many problems arise within the organization. It is called 'abnormality'. It is easy to understand that normality is a structure in which team members are in charge, but if an abnormality occurs, the team leader (manager) must intervene and resolve it. Chief executive officers are responsible for overall game-changing decision making and organizational command and control. In this way, the subject of the act of returning abnormality to normal is the manager, and the subject of the act of denying the reality for a better future shape is the management.

The manager's role is to prevent the organization from being pushed downward from its current position and to maintain its shape in the daily trembling. Management's role is to create selective and operational tremors and artificial and challenging changes to the organization in order to take the whole organization held by managers to the next level. If so, the ability to solve problems for occurrence-type and setting-type problems is the most necessary ability to be promoted to become a manager or to become a CEO.

As such, Toyota's focus on problem-solving is to provide a "field" that fosters one new employee as a manager and a manager. However, the ability to discover problems is to focus on 'visualization' in all areas in order to create a 'structure in which problems are revealed' because you cannot spend all of your time searching for problems every day. If you only know the problem, you work with the consciousness that someone can solve it.

This is a very deep perception, as many companies taboo the problem itself. If everyone is rebuked by their boss for having a problem, they try to hide the problem. This makes it difficult to visualize the problem, and the solution becomes more difficult. In places where managers or CEOs can't even notice, in places where management is weakest, problems erupt like lava bursts. Then, the manager or the CEO thinks that such a problem has arisen because of lack of control and strengthens management control. The vicious cycle begins.

On the other hand, Toyota takes it for granted that there is a problem. If there are no problems, there is no reason for an administrator to exist. Every day, a business site that remains intact requires only an operator and a boss. But there can be no such company. That is why the job and position of manager was born. This is the reason for their existence. It is natural that problems arise. Therefore, Toyota executives have the idea that rather than reprimand for the occurrence of a problem, they should reprimand for not solving the problem.

A culture that grows into talent through problem solving and reflection

So, who has to solve the problem? Of course they are managers. In many companies, it is a serious error in this regard to see the subject of problem solving as a "worker" or a front-line "practitioner". It will be difficult for the management to lean on the coincidence of "doesn't a young person have any fresh ideas?" to new employees at a meeting. In order for management to proceed smoothly, it is time to give a role appropriate to human nature or growth stage. Let's take a look at it.

Simplifying the stage of growth when a person enters the workplace can be expressed in one sentence:

"Follow him, help him, work with him, and finally replace him."

Perhaps the new employee doesn't know well about the company's business and culture. Therefore, the first thing a new employee can do is to follow the rules and learn little by little while following his boss. At this stage, the required competence is attitude, or attitude. As they get to know the job little by little, the new employee helps the boss's assistant and routine tasks. When he has accumulated some experience, he will work as a team with his senior and his boss. The competencies needed at this stage are skills, skills, and when they work together, when the boss moves to a different department or higher position, he finally takes over. The competency required at this stage is knowledge. Because by applying knowledge to work, we can achieve excellent results. Knowledge workers are born, including new standards of judgment accumulated through long experience and trial and error, commonly expressed as wisdom.

Following him, helping him, and working with him, they achieve today's goals. But to be a manager, you can't just play a role with the skills that allow you to do the job. It requires experience and knowledge as an ability to solve problems. Then, before becoming a manager, discover problems, come up with different ideas to solve them, and try them out. Through these efforts, even if it is not always successful, it will have the ability to respond to new situational changes or problems through trial and error. In accordance with this growth stage, a virtuous cycle of so-called situational leadership is possible by adjusting the ratio of instruction and support.

Toyota says this.

"It doesn't even have to be 100 points. 60 is good, so try it first."

In this word, there is a deep meaning of 'grow, not success'. There is, of course, a warning that a person who has continued to experience success only from a low position can cause a fatal failure to the company if he reaches a higher position later on. And it is because humans who have gone through trial and error can assess the failures of subordinates from the right perspective and lead a culture of learning from failures.

It is difficult to see that creative challenges will be activated in the culture of being fired for one failure. Could it be that companies such as Toyota Motor Co., who tolerate failure or Honda Motor Co., which promote failure, by selecting and rewarding "Failure King of the

Year," can create a culture that challenges, thinks, and acts!

Whether it is a 'occurrence type problem' or a 'setting type problem', it is to challenge and reflect on the problem to be solved to move forward and grow. Another important term comes up here, which is 'reflection'. It has been said that the definition of the problem is the gap between the goal and the phenomenon. To solve that goal, we find the problem that is the cause of the problem, and implement it through action tasks to solve it. The result obtained is called performance. This activity to identify the gap between achievements and goals is called 'reflection'. Even if the performance did not reach the goal, through accurate reflection, people and organizations can start on the basis of performance that is the result obtained from one challenge, rather than starting from scratch. By repeating that cycle of execution and reflection, we can finally achieve our goal. The definition of problem and reflection can be summarized as follows.

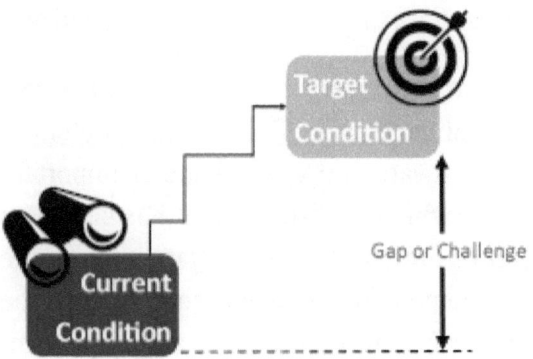

People can grow by repeating the process of setting goals, executing them, reflecting on them, and re-challenging. People with such problem-solving skills become managers and strive to make work easier and more comfortable for employees. Toyota's managers are the ones who focus most of their time on improvement, and the CEO is responsible for determining the direction of the entire organization and making decisions to make it better.

Problem solving and human resource development through The three reals

Toyota's management emphasizes "3reals"

It has a very profound meaning when it comes to accuracy. 3reals, which means 'see the real thing in the real scene and grasp the real fact', is a concept that has already been spread all over the world, and it is difficult to understand even though it is difficult to practice. But it seems I feel a little uncomfortable with Toyota's 3reals, which requires that the CEO, who has to make big and big decisions, has to look into the field every day. It seems that there are many cases where they think that it is the job of the factory manager or that it is something that can be left to the executives.

However, it is easy to understand if you look at the structure of decision making, a major task of managers. It is often said that the situation should be considered when making decisions. After all, in order to make correct management judgments, it is necessary to clearly know the external situation and the internal level. Instead of relying on reports or documents to know properly, you have to look at the real thing on the spot and grasp the reality. In that respect, 3reals is a powerful tool, and it seems that tools such as Enterprise Resource Planning (ERP) are used as a means of 3reals.

Toyota is pursuing both problem solving and human resource development within the organization by repeating the process of identifying the phenomenon based on 3reals, replacing occurrence-type problems or setting-type problems with targets. And it has a structure that fits well with the stage of human growth or the stage of growth of roles within the organization. Their philosophy is expressed in these words.

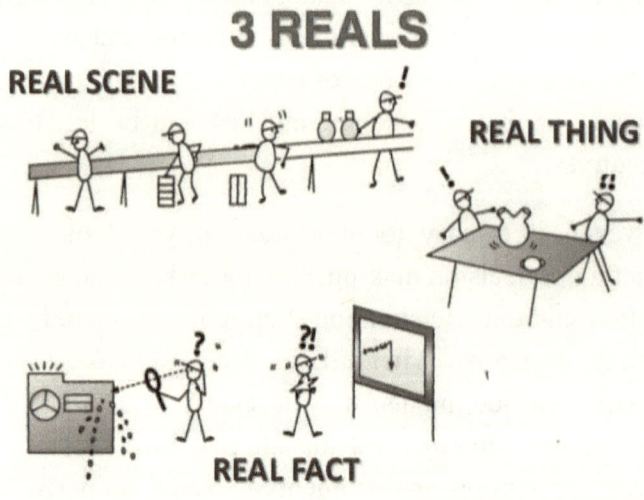

"Humans do not grow by success, but by growing they finally succeed."

So, what is the atmosphere of an organization that grows people? Meeting culture can be seen as a barometer. Due to respect for tradition and authority and the experience of success achieved by the boss, it is common for our meetings to speak only to the boss, while the rest remain silent and write down the words of the boss in their notebooks. In fact, this trend is not only the responsibility of the company, but is also mentioned as a pronoun of sharp contrast when comparing the so-called Western society, Eastern society, and Korean society. I would like to focus not on which one is good or bad, but on which method is more desirable to cultivate people who can draw conclusions that meet the needs of the times in the 21st century.

A creative and autonomous person is a person who can control himself. To do that, you need to know how to think for yourself. Be a person who knows how to think and do what is right, not do things right. You have to be able to think for yourself and say it. In terms of corporate culture, it also means that employees should think for themselves and provide opportunities and fields to freely speak their thoughts. You can grow by thinking, speaking, and taking action, reflecting on the gap between your goals and achievements, and re-creating new action plans.

Poster showing the value of Toyotism, which simultaneously pursues problem solving and human resource development. (Source:): Improve the Work, Develop the People

In order for people to be immersed, they need a field where they can make their own decisions and reflect on the results of their actions. Even in order to prepare such a place, it can be said that a project-type work structure is desirable. And it can be said that Toyota's "A3 culture" is what made this process objective and efficient. In the next chapter, let's take a look at Toyota's efficient corporate culture, which saves all documents such as plans and reports with one A3.

Chapter 12.

Toyota's A3 Culture for Maximum Efficiency

A3 report as a work improvement technique for problem solving

How do we usually use PowerPoint to write a proposal or plan? It would be common to make many slides in the order of purpose, background, market analysis, concept, etc. However, it is also true that such a large amount of material does not receive very good reviews from those who review it.

Saburo Kawabuchi, who served as the head of the Japan Football Association, evaluated Toyota's A3 culture by telling the story of the launch of the J-League, Japan's top football league.

This is the story when President Kawabuchi started the J-League. At that time, many proposals came in from companies wishing to participate in the league, and Kawabuchi said that.

"Toyota (Nagoya Grampus) was the most well-made material among the plans. The proposal they submitted was only two pages. It was written only that they wanted to participate in the J-League in this way. It was enough because what was needed was concise and clearly described.

On the other hand, plans of other companies are uselessly thick, but the contents are only poor ones! It was difficult to read because unnecessary content was written hesitantly. What was interesting is that most of the proposals summarized the "J League ideology" at the beginning. Originally, the ideology of the J-League was made by me. I don't even remember teaching it to others. How many plans are there that show meaningless words! Explaining the J-League ideology to the J-League founder... .... . This is the case for preaching in front of the Buddha. However, I myself also make these mistakes well. Readers don't think, they create and wrap up a self-centered presentation document. At that time, the sentences were usually lengthened. What is really important? If you enjoy it enough, it will be a more concise and easy-to-read proposal... ... ."

As shown above, Toyota's principle is to organize the plan into one A3 (or A4) sheet. The A3 paper is divided into four, and in each area, only the key points such as business purpose, planning content, execution plan, and sales strategy are summarized concisely. However, this culture is not only applicable to the proposal. All types of business documents, such as proposals, reports, meeting materials or minutes, materials used for business discussions, presentation materials, schedule confirmation lists, and high-density interview documents, are organized into one sheet.

In particular, Toyota, which rotates the CAPD's work cycle, constantly visualizes problems and improves problems that are revealed. One of the work improvement techniques for solving this problem is the "A3 Report" itself.

When looking at the general report's report and preparation instructions, it is a rule to fill in the following 8 items.

It consists of eight items:

① theme

② background of theme

③ identification of phenomena

④ goal setting

⑤ factor analysis

⑥ countermeasures and implementation

⑦ implementation result and development

⑧ reflection and future tasks

The main feature is that it does not end with a simple method of writing, but can develop problem-solving skills through the process of thinking in the order of writing documents. First of all, thinking in this style makes the problem clear. This is because the 8 items described above correspond to 8 steps as they are, and these 8 steps are the order of problem solving as they are. After entering the company, thinking and working in accordance with this style will naturally develop problem-solving skills. So, this way of thinking is called 'A3 Thinking Method'.

On the left side of the A3 report, items before project implementation, such as goal setting, current situation analysis, and factor analysis, are written. And on the right side, write what you learned, what you didn't do, and what you can standardize or deploy across the whole company.

By thinking in this order, priorities can be determined, preparations, etc. become clear, and improvement can be continued as a daily routine.

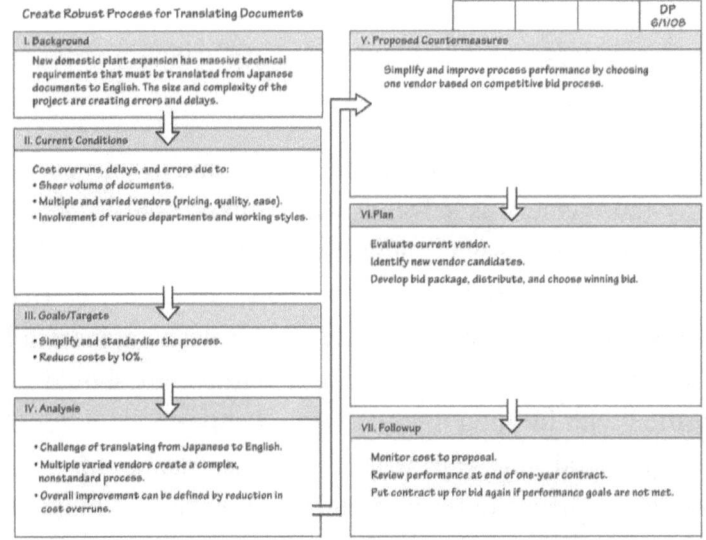

Sample of Toyota's one-page report

8 steps of A3 thinking method and A3 report writing method

First of all, the theme corresponding to the title of the project should be expressed in one word so that the overall view of the content can be seen. Whether it is an occurrence type problem or a setting type problem, the gap between the desired state or appearance and the phenomenon is a problem, so it is important to be able to easily understand what members are trying to do by clearly revealing these problems.

After the theme is selected, the background or purpose of why the theme was selected will be expressed in detail. Often, the reason why inductive improvement activities, such as that it will be better than now, are mainly carried out is because of the lack of urgency or desperateness for a clear goal in the background or purpose. It should be written with in mind that the desired appearance is set in advance and the gap with the current situation is a problem. Then, the background or purpose that must be achieved to a certain level and forever becomes clear. Therefore, the task that is followed by execution has a distinct result of deductive thinking.

The next step and the process that Toyota values most in problem-solving is the identification of the status quo. It can be said that 70% of success or failure depends on identifying the status quo. In fact, it is also the stage where I do the most rework when I conduct theme training related to this in Nagoya with Korean company employees. It is common to see a lot of cases listing problems right at this stage. However, grasping the phenomena is a step to reveal the current way or flow of work as it is. Write the current method as it is, divided into the smallest unit without value judgment.

Fourth, when it comes to goal setting, you need to clarify what, by when, and to what extent to improve. When setting a theme, a desirable state or appearance has already been assumed, so it is better to identify gaps that have become clear by analyzing the phenomenon and set them as goals. A goal such as a 30% increase in productivity, a 50% reduction in lead time, and a 30% improvement in throughput must be clear to everyone in order to be convinced and sprint to achieve it.

To do this, the definition of the desired state is very important. When it comes to clarifying the desired conditions to be reached, such as the level to compete with other companies or to take the lead in the market, the goal can be placed in the heart of everyone. And the effort to achieve such a goal and the consistency of the deadline can be obtained on the basis of a proper understanding of the phenomenon. If everyone sighs or cynically responds as soon as they hear a goal, it is not because the goal is not justified, but because it is often the goal presented without a clear diagnosis of the company's current level and foundation.

In the fifth step, factor analysis, the problem and the true cause are analyzed. The problem is the gap between the phenomenon and the ideal, and the true cause is the cause of the problem. To find the true cause, Toyota mainly uses methodologies such as 5why and cause&effect diagrams, which say 'Repeat why 5 times'. The most important principle of action at the stage of identifying the phenomenon and the stage of interpreting this factor is the so-called 3reals, which is intended to fundamentally prevent the tabletop theory.

Teamwork shines in the sixth step, measures and implementation. There are many people talking about the experiences of the countermeasures meeting, in which a problem arises and the members of the relevant departments gather and hold a meeting, and the contents of the presentation were all explanatory materials that were not the responsibility of their own department. It is much more productive for the people to come together and focus on solving the problem at the time of hours of diligence and time to create a statement that it is not my responsibility. Whether it is an occurrence type problem or a setting type problem, if it is the most unfavorable to the evaluation to be still in front of it, everyone will move forward toward problem solving. The execution at that time is to advance into the unknown world, so it cannot be perfect. That is why Toyota urges action and tolerates failure by saying,'Don't pursue perfection, even if 60 is good, try and think.'

Collaboration and teamwork that attempts to achieve the best overall result by cross-organizational review of countermeasures for the true cause found through 5why can be valuable in a culture that encourages problem solving and promotes failure. It would be no exaggeration to say that the effect of brain-storming, where people who decided to solve the problem gathered and discussed, made today's Toyota. A person's ability or knowledge is determined by the will to do. Therefore, the size of ability and knowledge is also important, but the most important thing is the will and direction of positive (+) or negative (-) orientation. On this cultural basis, creative ideas pour out.

The biggest feature of preparing a plan is that the person in charge and the deadline are clearly set. By doing this, execution power is increased. Recently, there is a movement to prepare a countermeasure from the noun form to the verb form. Avoid abstract expressions and write countermeasures with concrete verb forms. By the way, more specifically, Toyota expresses "from verb to action," which specifies what to do as a unit of action. To give an example to the students studying this, it can be expressed as reading and writing 3 pages of an English book, let's study to improve their skills. From a noun form to a verb form, and from a verb form to an action form, the more concrete you have, the higher your execution ability. Here, write who and when, and be sure to confirm.

Seventh, in implementation results and development, it is the step of measuring the performance of the activity. If the results obtained can be developed across the enterprise, we actively propose transverse development. Toyota's strength is that it has hardware (group self-study group, case presentation contest, etc.) that can disseminate one success story at the fastest speed not only within the organization but also throughout the supply chain including partners.

Finally, it is the stage of reflection and future tasks. Toyota often says "where there is no standard, there is no improvement." It is natural to say that where there is no "standard" to distinguish between normal and abnormal, there cannot be "improvement" that is better than the present. If this is expressed as a principle of action, it can be expressed as "improvement by standard," and as a result, it can be said that Toyota makes improvements that change standards.

To explain the cycle of this is this. Every job has a clear job definition and process criteria. Workers must adhere to the rules and standards. Nevertheless, if there is a problem, raise it as an improvement object. People concerned gather to improve. Create new standards, standards. Workers must adhere to the standard.

By repeating such a cycle, Toyota's improvement activities to raise the standard are possible without shaking in the form of repetition of 'maintenance + improvement'. Standardization is like a land we have to step on to support the present and move forward. "If you are not standing firmly on the ground, do not leap. It will surely hurt" that Toyota and the lean companies understand.

As they have been consistently doing improvement activities for 80 years since their establishment, they realize that improvement activities are, in the end, double investment. Under the banner of Daichi Ohno, the founder of the Toyota Production System (TPS), it has been a decade of rushing for "Mudatori (elimination of non-value added work). Why is it not 'excluded' from work that is not value-added from the beginning, but 'removed'

Why solve the problem behind the scenes? Can't it be possible to "exclude" the problem in advance from a higher class? Through these questions, the Toyota people changed their "definition of work" and moved 'from after-care to prevent'.

Chapter 13.

Don't take countermeasures after death, but prevent them

The work of a general company follows the flow of development-production preparation-production-sale. Smaller problems occurring upstream of this flow become more and more serious as they flow downstream, resulting in huge losses, so there are terms such as 'micro management' or 'root management' in the workplace.

The so-called 'Heinrich's Law' expresses the importance of micro management. Statistically, if one serious safety accident occurs, 29 minor accidents have occurred with the same cause before that, and about 300 experiences of exposure to risk already exist. Therefore, it is also the logic that a major accident can be prevented by properly grasping those signs and taking thorough preparations. Toyota and Lean Company are responding to small changes through techniques such as so-called change point management or 3H management. 3H management refers to a micro management technique following the Japanese acronyms of Hajimete, Henkou, and Hisashiburi, which represent 'new, changed, and intermittent'.

The importance of upper stream management or root management can also be explained by the so-called 1:10:100 rule. Joseph M. Juran, a world-class quality expert, said that there are three categories of cost to solve a problem and secure quality: 'prevention cost', 'correction cost' and 'failure cost'. 'Prevention cost' is the cost for quality control activities or training to prevent defects in quality from the beginning. "Correction cost" is the cost of inspecting a product, finding defects or defects, and taking countermeasures, that is, the cost of maintaining the quality level by formally evaluating and correcting the quality. 'Failure cost' refers to the cost used to resolve a failure caused by a defective product or service being brought to the market and delivered to customers.

In addition, Joseph Juran stated that the relative ratio of these three costs was 1:10:100. In fact, a survey of this ratio at the IBM business in Rochester, USA found it to be 1:13:92. Therefore, in order to minimize the quality cost, it can be seen that it is best to eliminate all possible defects and defects in advance in the design stage. The proportion of these activities can be expressed as the proportion of preventive activities: corrective activities: failure countermeasure activities. Toyota people, who have been working on failure countermeasures (Mudatori) to solve problems for a long time, raise their heads and look at the upstream process. I will briefly introduce the prevention techniques implemented by Toyota.

Front loading and vertical start-up to solve the problem from the front

Toyota attaches great importance to "early detection and early resolution" of problems. This is because most of product cost and quality are determined in the early stages of design and upstream processes. 'Front loading' is the process of detecting and solving problems that may arise by predicting future changes as early as possible. This frontloading accident can also be applied to the service industry. By anticipating and preparing for problems that may arise in the future, related service systems, processes, and systems are improved. By doing so, things are avoided from getting worse and better.

"Vertical start-up" means realizing maximum production as early as possible immediately after mass production starts. In general companies, various problems occur after the start date of mass production, and the plant utilization rate is usually lowered. As the problem is solved, the utilization rate gradually increases, and an S curve is drawn that achieves full production only after a certain period of time. However, Toyota's idea of a vertical start-up is that the utilization rate should be brought to 100% from the very day of mass production. This also becomes a task of course to solve the problem in advance. If this is expressed as a picture, it is as follows.

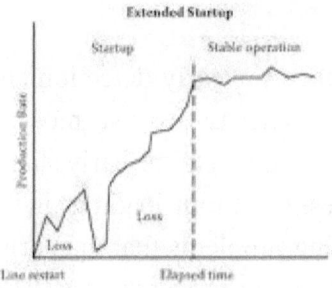
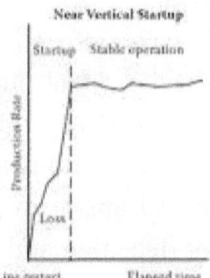

The reason vertical start-up is necessary is that it cannot respond to initial demand when the utilization rate of production is low. The product lifecycle is getting shorter and more competitive in today's world.

The reasons why vertical start-up is not possible are as follows.

-There was a problem in the production process, and a problem occurred in the production line.

-The skill level of operator or preparation replacement is low. We have not been able to secure workers who have learned the work of the product.

-The optimum value of the facility setting was not found.

-There was a problem in the procurement of parts.

Originally, this problem must be solved in the production preparation stage, but the reality is that many companies do not. For a vertical start-up, Toyota is trying to find and solve problems early through frontloading that goes back to the development stage, which is an earlier stage.

As thoughts reach the stage of development, there is an important inflection point here.

Toyota's efforts to solve problems that arise during the transcription (production) process of ideal information are well known. Customer's claim, an effort to reduce the cost of failure. In addition, efforts to resolve defects and troubles in the process within the factory, that is, efforts to reduce judgment costs. It is no exaggeration to say that Toyota's improvement methods and tools related to these two tasks have been benchmarked by companies around the world. That is why the preconceived notion that the Toyota method is a topic of interest only in the manufacturing industry was formed.

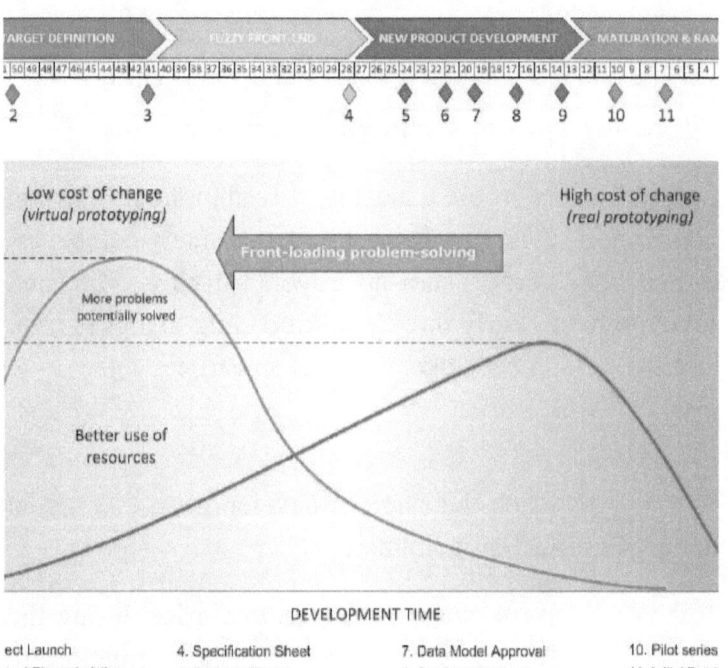

However, the Toyota people, working according to the above-mentioned trend, finally came to the conclusion that they should reduce the cost of prevention by preventing them. Here, the subject of the activity changes. This is because until before, 'people working in the transcription process of ideal information were the targets, but problem solving in the development stage was the target of 'people working in the process of 'creating ideal information'. Now, by encompassing the domains targeting the service industry and white-collar, Toyotism has been expanded into thinking systems and methodologies that can be used in all industries and all business areas, such as so-called lean design, lean engineering, and lean processes, and has established itself in companies around the world. .

Already in the 1990s, Toyota made tremendous achievements through this frontloading. Development period was cut in half, development cost was reduced by 30%, and wasteful activities such as design changes were reduced by more than 90%. In 1995, while other competitors had 36 to 48 months of development lead time, Toyota had 24 months of capability. After that, it succeeded in reducing it back to 18 months in 1996 and to 13 months in 1998.

There are likewise three directions of efforts to reduce non-valued work in the process of "creating ideal information". First, there are 'to make information visible and easy to understand', 'to share information in real time', and 'to make a database of know-how (tacit knowledge)'. Now let's find out through specific techniques.

Prevention technique GD³ in the development stage

GD³ (GD Cube) is a technique that prevents the occurrence of nonconformities in advance when doing 'improved design' based on existing products. Good Design, Good Discussion, and Good Dissection or Good Design-review). The process of creating the value of development is a very creative activity because it is the 'creation of ideal information', which we have discussed above. In addition, the activity of preventing problems that have not yet occurred is in itself the same as walking in the dark. It is not easy to put "forecasting or predicting" what will happen within the framework of management. However, the technique of "discovering" a problem can be generalized or generalized and put into the framework of the science of management. In that sense, this GD³ can also be called a problem finding technique.

Some people have excellent predictive ability, predictive ability, and insight. It can be seen that it is the conversion of tacit knowledge, which is the ability to become such an individual's characteristic, into formal knowledge. Good Design is a method of thinking of creative ideas, and Good Discussion and Good Dissection are methods for finding problems.

DRBFM, a creative prevention technique

DRBFM (Design Review Based-on Failure Mode) is also a creative prevention technique developed by Toyota Motor Company. It is a problem-solving technique that is now mandated not only by Toyota, but also by Toyota Group and its partners. It is also a technique that I am actively introducing to domestic companies by inviting advisor Kokubo from the director of the Denso Institute of Technology every year at my global business consulting.

In a narrow sense, DRBFM is a method to detect potential factors (mainly new, changed, intermittent) that may cause quality problems in advance and prevent them in advance. In a broader sense, a system that reviews all manufacturing processes such as quality and process in advance to prevent problems that may occur from the design stage to the mass production process, and reviews and improves all these processes even after delivery to customers. Say the methodology.

The procedure is the same as the Failure Mode and Effects

Analysis (FMEA), but it is characterized by thorough concentration of the subject of review on the change point. Experts gather to derive problems and solve them by matching points where changes occur, such as parts or functions that are newly adopted (new), changed parts or functions (changes), parts or functions that are used in the past but reused after a long time (intermittent).

Chapter 14.

Toyota's New Values, TNGA

TNGA, a new platform to run Toyotism

'TNGA (Toyota New Global Architecture)'.

This is the skeleton of a new future that Toyota draws. Why are they trying to build this? Why didn't they give it up?

It means that, as all companies realize, the way of working in the upstream stages (development, design stage, and ideal information creation process) that determines 70-80% of added value determines competitiveness. In that sense, TNGA symbolizes a comprehensive sense of "work" to create a "better car" pursued by Toyota. It is not simply a renewal of engines or platforms, it can be seen as a renewal of the company-wide working method, including from the automobile development process to the manufacturing process. When the TNGA Planning Department was established, the following five points were raised.

1.Improvement of product power (product power is a marketing term that is evaluated by multiplying selling power (product power) by selling power (sales power = distribution ability)): through low center of gravity that lowers the height of the hood by changing the skeleton of the car, visibility and athletic performance Raises. It was introduced from a new car released in 2015. The powertrain was also renewed.

2. Efficiency through grouping development: Mid- to long-term product line-ups are set, and units and driving positions are set in advance as "architecture". Based on that, grouping development is carried out to improve efficiency through'Commonization' of parts.

3. Manufacturing innovation: Partners, procurement, production technology, and technology are united to realize a simple and easy-to-make unit.

4. Global standard orientation: Not only for Toyota, but also for global standards adopted by other manufacturers.

5. Procurement strategy linked with TNGA: We secure competitiveness by arranging units of multiple vehicle types and placing orders globally, regardless of vehicle type, region, or time.

As is well known, development of next-generation models has been underway under this policy. According to Toyota's announcement, the body stiffness of the new platform has been increased by 30-65% compared to the previous model by reviewing the skeleton. It began to be applied to the 2015 Prius, and was sequentially applied to compact cars, large cars, and FR cars (front-engine rear-wheel drive cars), and in 2020, about half of the global sales were produced by cars that adopted the TNGA platform.

Toyota sought to realize a "cool design" by lowering the engine's mounting position at TNGA, lowering the vehicle's center of gravity and improving driving performance, while also lowering the height of the bonnet. For engines with rear intake and front exhaust, the exhaust pipe from the front of the engine passes under the engine and leads to the rear. In contrast, for engines with front intake and rear exhaust, it is easy to lower the mounting position of the engine because the exhaust pipe does not pass under the engine.

Conventionally, even when a platform is newly designed, it was common to design on the premise that an existing engine or transmission is mounted. Conversely, even when redesigning the engine, there were many cases where it was designed to be mounted on an existing platform. This means that if an existing platform or an existing engine is premised, it itself becomes a design constraint.

For example, even if an attempt is made to lower the mounting position of the engine to lower the center of the vehicle, such as the TNGA, there are naturally limitations given the dimensions and structure of the existing engine or transmission, and the arrangement of the exhaust pipe. In order to break through this limitation, it is necessary to pursue a 'overall optimal' in all the elements that make up the vehicle, not the 'partial optimum' design method of only the engine or only the body.

As such, an example of pursuing a "ideal structure" by linking all the parts that make up a vehicle is Matsuda's next-generation technology, "SKYACTIV". Mazda aims to achieve a level of performance that has not been achieved until now by simultaneously renovating all vehicle configuration technologies such as engines, transmissions, and bodywork, and further pursuing the overall optimization rather than individual optimum.

However, I thought that it would be difficult to introduce reforms that simultaneously renew all the elements of a car because there are many types of vehicles and many types of engines and transmissions in large companies like

Toyota. In fact, when the person in charge of Matsuda introduced SKYACTIV, "Mazda is a small-scale company, so we pursued the strengths that can be used. In a big company, it will be difficult to renovate everything at the same time." However, Toyota challenged it. The real meaning of TNGA is that the world's largest automaker has undertaken an all-renewal reform.

Toyotism is not a reverse idea, but common sense of our time

In short, I explained that Toyota secures quality and cost in a preventive and aggressive manner through these preventive techniques. This proactive mindset further requires a radical change in the way people view the work of the people working in each sector. For example, when you ask a person working in the quality control department, "What is your job?", other companies often answer "inspection." However, the definition of work in Toyota's quality control department is "to get rid of inspections." They believe that it is their role to plan the process so that good products can be produced without inspection, to create standards or tools for quality inspection, and to guide suppliers. The idea that it is not a job to prevent the leakage of defects found through inspections or to follow up on customer complaints shows that we understand the nature of prevention.

Likewise, if you ask someone who works in the maintenance department, "What is your job?", if there is a case of answering "fixing the machine", Toyota responds "to prevent the machine from breaking down." When asked what the purpose of cleaning is, they say, "not to make it clean," but to "to keep it from becoming dirty." Cleaning isn't about getting rid of dirt, it's about identifying potential problems and keeping things clean from getting dirty. Everyone will have the experience of being careful about their own behavior in very clean places. That is the purpose of cleaning, and the intention and purpose of influencing human thoughts and actions through cleaning.

It is often said that when talking about Toyota's culture, they often think backwards, but once you understand the principles of Toyotism, you can see that everything is not reversed. So they say so consistently, "We just do what is taken for granted."

What I will continue to say in this book is that, in the end, the paradigm that Toyota shows is 'common sense demanded by our time'. Because we are living in a transitional period, and still living under the powerful influence of Fordism, what they do seems to overturn common sense and only seem to be thinking backwards.

Lastly, in Part 3, I would like to examine the paradigm and how the organizations that understand and implement Toyotism as a way of working, that is, Lean Enterprises, have changed the world together.

PART 3.

Toyotism, work itself changes

Despite the explanation that Toyotism is a very natural "common sense" for solving the mission of the times we live in, strangely negative words about the introduction and implementation of Toyotism are overflowing.

Even if cited, they say, 'Even though many companies have benchmarked the Toyota method, no company has performed as much as Toyota', or 'It is not correct for the Toyota method, which is a management technology, because the industry (proprietary technology) is different.' There is a reason I emphasized in Part 1 that Toyota is different from many other Japanese companies.

Even when many companies see the Toyota method in person, there is a strong perception that "this is possible because it is Japanese." However, as a result of conducting a lot of training in China while visiting Toyota suppliers in China, I found that it can be applied to all industries and companies.

Then, how about companies that have succeeded in applying and adapting Toyotism?

The answer can be found by looking at how the United States, who defined and spread Toyotism as Lean, perceived it, what companies have inherited its value, and what new trends have been created.

Chapter 15.

The Revolution of the Timely Production System (JIT)

Toyota's JIT production method outpaced the US automobile industry

In the 1970s and 1980s, when the American manufacturing industry was struggling with Japanese companies, Toyota was on a completely different path. The manufacturing technology that supported Toyota's phenomenal success is now known all over the world under the concept of "Jit in Time". The JIT production system has been an important event in the history of manufacturing management.

Most of the concepts represented by JIT were realized by Daichi Ono of Toyota Motor Company. Toyota's president Kiichiro Toyota said, "Catch the United States within three years. Or the Japanese automobile industry will not survive." He started innovating in 1945. At that time, the difference in productivity between the US and Japanese automobile industries was 10 times. Of course, Toyota didn't catch up with the US in three years. But, as we all see now, it was the first step in which Toyota's goals were ultimately achieved and triggered some of the most fundamental changes in industry and management. Ono recognized that the only way to compete with the United States was to eliminate the cause of the differences in productivity that existed between the two countries. However, it was possible only by boldly removing unnecessary parts (non-value-added work and non-value-added work) with the goal of cost reduction. He uses the concept of autonomation to engage in activities to eliminate all nonconformities in quality problems, while pursuing JIT, which produces only 'what is needed, when needed, and as much as necessary' as he learned in supermarkets in the United States.

At the time, in the eyes of researchers at American automakers, Toyota's approach seemed to be the opposite of everything. The U.S. regards work preparation time as fixed and tries to solve it with an optimized lot size (Lot Size, which means the size of the lot that can minimize production cost in the production system, i.e. the number of processing at a time). did. Toyota achieves the ultimate production of 'one piece flow' (a method of producing one by one) through ceaseless efforts to eliminate or reduce the changeover time altogether. The US viewed delivery dates as external constants and tried to optimize production schedules to meet them. Toyota knew that delivery deadlines were negotiable with customers, and worked to integrate marketing and manufacturing processes to create a production schedule that did not require sudden changes.

In addition, the United States took for granted the irregular delivery method from the supplier and tried to calculate the optimal order quantity in relation to the logistics cost. Toyota has entered into long-term contracts with a handful of suppliers to enable regular delivery. While the U.S. accepted poor quality as inevitable and established elaborate inspection procedures, Toyota worked to ensure that quality requirements were recognized by both suppliers and internal workers outside the factory, and tools were created and deployed to maintain them.

Manufacturing engineers in the United States did their best to embrace the specifications made by the designers and adapt them to the manufacturing process, while Toyota's manufacturing and design engineers worked together to create designs that were easy to make. Like this, everything looked the opposite. Probably the readers may have felt similarly, but the same is true for changing "American companies" to "Korean companies".

In order to realize such JIT production, Ono aims to

equalize production, secure spare production capacity, shorten changeover (work preparation) time, multi-functional training and rotation work, total quality management, kanban method and The same tools and methodologies were created and realized. It is true that since the 1990s, many companies have made great efforts to benchmark these techniques, and it is true that the manufacturing competitiveness of many companies has been so advanced.

However, it is clear that Toyotism thinking, including JIT, is not a simple procedure or technique. Rather, it is a consistent and well-defined management strategy. Toyotism should be viewed as a collection of attitudes, philosophy, priorities, and methodologies toward work. It has the insight that demonstrates creative and powerful power by allowing one person and one person in the office and factory to work while conscious of customer satisfaction. They have long defined 'the next process is the customer'. This means that all of the people in the next process that take over the results of my work are my customers. That is, it is an order to satisfy them.

The emergence of Lean companies benchmarking the Toyota method

The question of whether Toyota's system can be transferred from Toyota to the United States was the biggest challenge for early researchers. However, the conclusions of early researchers stated that these techniques have very high transferability. "I believe this approach can be easily transferred to other countries," said Dr. Richard Schonberger, who introduced JIT to the United States for the first time. (Omitted) Toyota-style production and quality control will also be effective in other environments." Yasuhiro Monden also stated in his book "Toyota Production System", "I am convinced that Toyota's production system can play a huge role in improving organizations in the United States and Europe." However, as readers know, Toyota's kanban is still far from universal, and in fact, it is true that it is only used by Toyota. Nevertheless, American companies fiercely benchmarked Toyota. Imitation, or, euphemistically, benchmarking was a standard practice for American companies in the 1980s. Some American companies have achieved the desired results, but most have not. They wanted to get all of what Toyota had achieved in decades in a short period of time. Shigeo Shingo, one of the founders of the TPS, cried out like this.

"Some people think Toyota wears a nice new outfit called the kanban method. So they go out and try to buy and wear a pair of identical clothes. But soon they realize they are too fat to wear them."

The name lean was like "Guess's 24-inch jeans," in which jealousy and envy can only be felt. Jeans that can't be worn unless you are a slender person!

I have a similar idea. If you can't adopt the Toyota method, it's because you're not capable. The most beautiful measure of Toyota's ability is the "stock" level. Those who teach the Toyota method often say "stock is bad" to emphasize that you have to do production that makes little stock. But in reality, the stock is 'flower'. Because a large quantity of inventory is the result of other problems (absence, breakdown, defect, shortage, etc.). So many companies become "farms" with flowers in stock, even though they are "factory" that make things.

Toyota runs factories, not farms. They dream of a creative office that draws the maximum output with the least input, not an office like a farm where work is stagnant and piled up. Companies with the same dream appeared. The number of people who sympathize and participate has increased. Before long, good-willed competitors also began to appear. Lean companies, which are shining in many industries, are now active. Now let's talk about it.

Chapter 16.

Tesla and Toyota, Partners for the Car of the Future

There is increasing interest in Tesla, an emerging company that has emerged as a representative of electric vehicles, and Toyota, a traditional powerhouse that is currently a representative of gasoline and hybrid vehicles. The prospect that the gasoline era is approaching the end. At this point, the trend is already taking place, as the next-generation future car, Tesla is pouring energy into electric cars, and Toyota is pouring power into hydrogen fuel cell cars. What is the future of automobiles?

Google's Ivanpa Solar Power Plant vs. Tesla's Supercharger Station

The automobile industry has always symbolized the

energy system after the Industrial Revolution, represented by the use of fossil fuels, and even defined the way people working in that energy system work. The way of working, symbolized by Fordism, was also a way of dealing with resources in the energy system in the form of oil and electricity. Unfortunately, the energy system that supported Fordism, which pursues infinite profits through mass production and mass consumption, is finite.

It is no exaggeration to say that the world in which we live now was built on oil. But a dangerous change is coming to that energy system. The signs of the depletion of oil are growing. To cope with such risks, countries around the world are working to change new alternative energies and energy systems including them. What is needed right now is an effort to slow the consumption of petroleum resources. As a result of such efforts, we watched the competition between hybrid and clean diesel, and saw the fall of diesel through the diesel gate of Volkswagen. Now, we are witnessing the competition between electric vehicles and hydrogen fuel cell vehicles, which are slightly ahead of them. It will be an interesting spectator.

What I want to emphasize in this book is the story of work and the way we work, so I would like to avoid direct references to Toyota's products or future strategies as much as possible.

However, it is clearly emphasized that the paradigm shift from Fordism to Toyotism and the change in the way of working is based on renewable energy and resource circulation in the energy system represented by oil and electricity, that is, a centralized and elitist way of thinking. It includes a shift to a decentralized, collaborative mindset and a way of working as a premise.

Take a look at the figure below. This is a picture of Ivanpa Power Plant (ISEGS), the world's largest solar power plant located in the Mojave Desert, California, USA.

The power plant was officially put into operation after a test operation in the second half of 2013 with investments from Google, NRG Energy, and Bright Source Energy. The power generation capacity of the Ivanpa solar power plant is about 400MW, capable of generating electricity for use by 140,000 households per year, and is composed of 300,000 solar reflectors and three 40-story towers that function as collectors. Currently, it is operating a 12% reduction. A reflector called a heliostat (a reflector that sends sunlight in a certain direction) automatically adjusts the angle according to the sun's movement and maximizes the efficiency of solar power generation. IT companies such as Google and Apple, which operate data centers with enormous power consumption, are very interested in power generation, and are advancing into eco-friendly energy businesses such as solar and wind power, which they use in terms of environmental protection. As we saw earlier, Google started operating the Ivanpa Solar Power Plant, the world's largest solar project in the Mojave Desert. Apple is operating a solar power plant with a capacity of 18 to 20 MW in the Nevada desert by setting a policy to cover the power required to operate its own data center using environmentally renewable energy. The Ivanpa Power Plant is said to have the effect of reducing 400,000 tons of carbon dioxide emissions per year.

Isn't it cool? Actually, it's not cool. I think that the Ivanpa power plant is highly likely to become an old fossil built on the basis of centralized and elitist Fordism in the fossil fuel era.

Then let's look at the picture below.

But think. Sunlight is everywhere on this planet. Do you really need to go into the desert to build a power plant, power transmission, and distribution? The era of supplier-centered Fordism is gone. Now is the era of Toyotism in which customers only need to make or supply what they need, when they need it, and as much as they need. Are there people in the desert who need energy? no. It is in the city. Wouldn't it be necessary to operate solar power generation facilities where they are located and wherever they are located only for the required capacity? That's why Tesla was able to offer a "lifetime free charge" at as many charging stations as needed at minimal cost. Is there another Lean Company the size of Tesla?

Lean Company, Tesla, who practices JIT

In fact, there were some negative views of electric vehicles in the current energy system and paradigm that "electricity itself is a by-product of oil". To make electricity, we have to run power plants with oil, but the question is whether it is eco-friendly. However, Tesla's JIT-type charging station using small-scale renewable energy will dispel that opinion. In addition, Tesla has released a patent for a supercharger for free to accelerate the spread of electric vehicles.

Also, from 2013, Tesla introduced a battery exchange system. If the rechargeable system takes about 90 minutes, this battery exchange system takes 15 minutes. It got closer to JIT. Currently, it is said that the cost of charging gasoline at gas stations is lower than the cost. However, there are also psychological barriers when new car owners receive used batteries.

I go one step further and imagine. Of course, the most expensive part of an electric vehicle is a battery. So, what if you sell only car bodies without batteries from the beginning? Vehicle prices could be cheaper than expected. From the time of shipment, the battery rental system is activated. If the battery runs out while driving with a rental battery installed, replace the entire battery at a nearby battery exchange. The battery exchange also receives rental batteries supplied by Tesla and only receives a fee for 90 minutes of charging and replacement. Information such as battery life and driving distance is collected by Tesla with sensors and unique numbers attached to the battery, and is used as feedback data for better battery research and development. It cannot but be a pleasant imagination.

On the other hand, Toyota seems to be putting more emphasis on hydrogen fuel cell vehicles. By revealing the car model "Mirai", they revealed their inner mind. In addition, Toyota has also released a related patent for free to accelerate the diffusion of hydrogen fuel cell vehicles. The experience of successfully collaborating in the hybrid-related market by revealing a hybrid patent would have been helpful. The idea of creating electricity based on hydrogen that exists indefinitely will emerge as a symbol of resource circulation and decentralized operation system as soon as safety issues such as the possibility of hydrogen explosion are solved.

As discussed in this way, the commonality between

Toyotism and Lean Companies is that they work in a way that minimizes the waste of resources based on decentralization and collaboration, not in a centralized and elitist manner. In fact, getting the maximum output with the minimum input is the basis of all management, but as it turns out, the essence of Toyotism is to minimize the waste of management resources and achieve maximum production. Not only the strategy, but also the way to achieve it should be 'lean'. In that sense, I think that Toyota and Tesla are not competitors, but partners that shape the future, and are firm builders of Toyotaism.

Google and Apple are investing in solar power generation projects in the form of building power plants in the desert, so I want to see their future more. The paradigm is not so easy. This is because what is now innovative and sustainable with an innovative paradigm are different. That doesn't mean Google's attempts aren't just bad. Now let's talk about Google.

Chapter 17.

New Paradigm Partners, Google and Toyota

Social change led by Google's self-driving car

Interest in self-driving cars is also hot. We want to help you understand self-driving cars through articles on Blotter.Net.

Google is by far the most advanced player in the autonomous vehicle technology competition. Google officially announced plans to develop autonomous vehicles in 2010. The early version of Google's self-driving car equipped with a camera, GPS, and various sensors on a Japanese car maker Toyota's Prius is famous.

Google even unveiled a prototype of an autonomous vehicle in December 2014. At the time, Google described the prototype as "an autonomous vehicle that is close to a real product." This means that the vehicle has melted the research over the past six years. Compared to the previous research self-driving car, the sensor equipment mounted on the car has been miniaturized, and various convenience functions have been added so that it can run on the actual road.

The sensor equipment mounted on the roof of Google's self-driving car is called "LiDAR". It is the core of Google's technology, which includes remote laser systems. Sound wave equipment, 3D cameras, and radar equipment are included. Riders measure the distance between objects and objects as if they were humans, and help them detect danger. Each sensor has a different role. The detectable distance also differs. For example, laser equipment measures distance using the principle that it collides with an object and reflects it. It is designed to detect all 360 degrees, and it reads information 1.6 million times per second. In addition, the 3D camera installed to look ahead is a technology that the vehicle is equipped with to understand the road situation in real time. The 3D camera increases the accuracy of distance measurement compared to photographing an object with a single camera. It is the same principle that a person detects distance with two eyes. The 3D camera is designed to detect up to 30m distance.

In addition, various equipment and technologies such as GPS and Google Maps are installed. The core of Google's autonomous vehicle technology is to reduce blind spots that cars cannot detect by utilizing various advanced sensor equipment according to purpose and function.

Google self-driving car

Ryosuke Izumida, the representative of Japan's GF Research and author of 《Google vs. Toyota》, foretold the disruption that autonomous vehicles will bring. It is believed that the meaning of auto insurance, the flow of targets or funds, and the industry structure will change due to the spread of autonomous vehicles. In addition, changes are inevitable in the regulation and operation of the supervisory authority, such as whether a driver's license is required. Self-driving cars, which will be the crystallization of information and communication technology, can be products sold by telecommunication companies rather than automobile companies. Basically, since electric vehicles use batteries as their main power source, fundamental changes will come to the supply chain of the existing automobile manufacturing industry. Electric vehicles can transform a city from an energy consumer to an energy storage function.

The outlook that it will bring about a big change in the above five areas prevails, and I have a view that it will make a big blow to the love-related industry, especially the hotel industry. The scene where lovers whisper love in a car while driving on a beautiful outer road is likely to be a tempting aspect above all else. I think cars will increasingly become a means of providing new illusions to humans. In an era where emotion is more important than reason, the value of 'fantasy' is much greater than 'function'. In any case, the society that self-driving cars will create in various senses will be distinctly different from the present society.

Google and Toyota lead the transition to a smart social system

Then, what is the reason Google is developing self-driving cars?

Earlier, it was said that the 21st century in which we live requires a new energy system and a way of working. It is easy to predict that a new energy system will eventually lead to a new social system. So, again, why is Google paying attention to cars? Izumida asks the question whether Google sees autonomous vehicles as the most important hardware in the transition from current social systems to new, smarter social systems.

Google already has a track record of conquering the system with Apple through hardware called smartphones. Perhaps Google has a big dream of contributing to the entire social system by dominating the hardware of smartphones and cars. Often, the confrontation between Apple and Samsung is expressed as "a war between software and hardware," but in reality it should be called "a confrontation between system and hardware". This is because Apple has succeeded in building an ecosystem. Samsung just sold the handset. If Apple and Samsung can see the success of a system product that combines hardware and service platforms, the same composition can be seen in Google and Toyota. At least, for Koreans, Samsung and Toyota are the strongest hardware players and are subject to common recognition as global leaders.

In that sense, in the recent environment that can be called a new industrial revolution and digital revolution of the automobile industry, Toyota's greatest threat can be said to be the emergence of emerging companies symbolized by Google. The biggest strength of Samsung, which has benchmarked Toyota and Toyota so far, is due to the fast lead time through vertical integration of the supply chain. It can be said that it has become an unrivaled two major mountain ranges in terms of operational excellence that can develop, produce, and sell new products faster than anyone else.

The battle between electric vehicles and hydrogen fuel cell vehicles over power sources is still a battlefield where the influence of hardware is exerted. However, the story of autonomous vehicles is very different. Like the aspect of the fight seen on a smartphone, this is a battlefield like a kind of mixed martial arts. It's a situation where you don't know who, when, and what technology will come out. Anyone can be an ally, and anyone can be an enemy. However, Toyota has only the Toyota Group. There is a possibility that the strength of the vertical series that followed only by looking at Toyota, including parts suppliers, would turn into a weakness. If that happens, there is a high possibility that it will not be Toyota vs. Google, but Toyota vs. the whole world.

There is a possibility that Apple's standalone camp fights against the world created by Google, eventually giving up 80% of the market. This is because Google also has the strengths of Toyota, and its scope is rather wider. Google is envisioning a "new social system including automobiles". On the other hand, Toyota is in the "paradoxical defensive force" of top-ranked companies, who have been conceived of a "new social system from automobiles," and now have to open their eyes and adapt to a new trend.

For example, if Tesla and Google, which have an integrated production system for automobile hardware, join hands, the damage to the existing automobile industry, including Toyota, will be beyond imagination. Ominous imaginations are creepy in that they sometimes become reality.

From another angle, you might want to savor the words of Jeremy Rifkin. In his book The Third Industrial Revolution, he stressed that "great economic transformation in history occurs when new communication technologies meet new energy systems." There is an amazing paradigm melted in these words.

Until Fordism became mainstream, that is, in the pre-industrial stage, the energy system was the power of animals symbolized by manpower or horsepower, and that was the communication method of transportation and communication. That's how people deliver letters or run words. In that sense, a new energy system that uses fossil fuels and automobiles that emerged in an era when transportation was communication was truly a major event in which "new energy systems and communication technologies" met. Cars have emerged as the protagonists of a new energy system, replacing wagons. In addition, it played a role in strengthening the exchange and communication of human society along with telephone and telegraph.

How about now? The self-driving car made by Google symbolizes the combination of a new energy system based on renewable energy and resource circulation and internet communication technology symbolized by smartphones.

In retrospect, Ford wasn't actually the first runner of the Industrial Revolution, nor was it a runner who enjoyed its glory to the end. However, the Ford Motor Company, established in 1903, rises to the top of the list in 1913, with the communication technology of automobiles, business models and conveyor systems that hold the icons of the era that connects transportation and communication. However, since 1931, when Alfred Sloan's GM, which reflects the needs of a variety of customers, allowed a turnaround, it has never been to the throne. Nevertheless, the paradigm of the industrialization era and "Fordism" as a way of working have thus determined the paradigm of the last 100 years. In other words, Ford and Fordism were the same for 19 years from 1913 to 1931, but from 1931 Ford and Fordism were separated.

The same explanation and prospects for Toyota are possible. Toyota is also not the first runner of the new industrial revolution, and there is no guarantee that it will continue to enjoy its position in the future. In 2006, when Toyota Motor Company rose to the world's No. 1 ranking, Toyota Motor Company and Toyotism attracted the attention of the world. And again 15 years passed. At some point, Toyota's competitors are changing to Google and Apple, which possess communication technology rather than automakers. The essence of this phenomenon may be the great economic transformation that the 'new energy system meets communication technology' will bring. If Toyota gives the initiative to Google or Apple, then the separation between Toyota Motor and Toyota will occur again.

However, Toyotism as a "paradigm and working method"

of the 21st century will be inherited by companies with more advanced ideas and methodology, and will enjoy 100 years as a symbol of our time. Obviously, we will be using quiet, clean and smart vehicles, vehicles connected to a horizontal and cooperative decentralized two-way network. This is also a strong reflection of Toyotism. This pattern shows that we are at the end of an economic era and on the threshold of a new era. We are living a transitional life. If you don't meet the paradigm shift with your whole body, it will disappear along with the relics of the old world. In that respect, the same goes for those working at Toyota Motor Company.

I tried to deal with the bold hypothesis in response to the prejudice that it would be a piece of praise for Toyota as it is a book about Toyota Motor Company and Toyotism, but in fact, I think that both Toyota and Google are partners that open a new era.

Google used Toyota's Prius and Lexus RX as prototypes for self-driving cars. As the author of this book, a smile comes out. Unlike Tesla, which has a hardware production base, what if Google, which does not have a hardware production base, has a strategy to sell self-driving cars in partnership with Toyota. If Google's shareholder capital and net profit are placed in the auto industry, Google already ranks third in the industry after Toyota and Volkswagen. It is a scene that can be said to be more threatening than Tesla, which is triumphantly.

On the one hand, it is worthwhile to think about the position of Korean companies in the future that Google, Toyota, and Tesla are opening up. We can imagine that Samsung and LG will establish themselves as two companies supporting human urban mobility combined with transportation and communication in the hardware area of smartphones and the hardware area of electric vehicles, respectively. It's not far from the future.

This is also the reason why Samsung and LG believe it is truly dangerous unless they cry out for creative management on the basis of their operational know-how and competitive advantage of fast speed. As mentioned earlier, advocating for a software company while giving up its strengths as a hardware manufacturing company can have the same result as winning a gold medal in Olympic archery just because of being a Korean. Going up on stage without proper preparation can have disastrous results. It can be beautiful enough to just participate and collaborate as an orchestra player. Of course, it would be even more wonderful to get into the position of conductor.

Chapter 18.

Toyotism in Germany, Industry 4.O

The wind of Industry 4.0 from Germany is spreading all over the world. A lot of people are paying attention to the point that it is said that the fourth industrial revolution is said. It's an amazing phenomenon. However, as we continue to emphasize, the phenomenon is not the cause. Just as waves are not the essence of the sea, the essence of the phenomenon of Industry 4.0, which spreads around Germany, lies in Toyotism.

The goal of Industry 4.0 is Toyotaism

The concept of Industry 4.0, which was outlined in 2011,

is very grand. The approximate meaning of this is that 'the factory solves the problems that the world faces', and in order to realize it, 'to pursue a smart factory through the cyber physical system'. To put it more simply, it upgrades the automation that combines IT and equipment such as PLC (Programmable Logic Controller), industrial robot, various machine tools, and transport equipment, which are currently used factory control devices. Therefore, the goal is to realize a very flexible production process that enables the entire factory to be completely networked, immediately prepares production plans according to demand, and completes production quickly. Technically, it means having a factory network that can be linked to any company's production facilities or management systems by using sensor technology, big data, virtual design technology, and communication technology. By doing so, it aims to achieve a smooth and efficient implementation of designs, configurations, orders, plans, production, and delivery that are different for each customer and product in a 'dynamic cell production' method.

Now, let's cut off the flesh and leave the skeleton of what Industry 4.0 is for. After all, in short, it is to give autonomy to the factory to solve problems of failures and defects, and to realize flexible production planning, production, and delivery that meet the diverse needs of customers. This is the purpose. The means are technologies that have grown rapidly in recent years, such as ICT and intelligent robots.

Yes. Industry 4.0 refers to the core concepts of Toyotism, Autonomation and JIT (Just In Time, a method of producing and delivering only what customers need, when they need it, and only as much as necessary).

And those who actually planned Industry 4.0 benchmarked the digital factory system named V-COMM and COMPASS developed and operated by Toyota. In the end, Industry 4.0 can be said to have sprung up in Germany through Toyota and Boeing, who are passionate about learning Toyota. V-COMM (Visual & Virtual Communication) is a system to shorten the period from development to production preparation and improve productivity and quality by reviewing interference and workability by creating 3D data from drawings in the design stage. Developed and applied in 1996. In addition, the Comprehensive Process Planning Assembly Simulation System (COMPASS) converts the time or part of each work element into a database, and verifies the balance of working time and the shortest walking distance between workers when there is a changeover due to model change, etc. As a system, it was already developed and applied in 2002.

Industry 4.0 is a trend, not a paradigm

As seen above, it can be said that the substance of Industry 4.0 is the body of armor such as ICT, intelligent robots, and sensors, which have developed rapidly since the 2000s, on the framework of the core idea of Toyotism. However, it's worth remembering that "the greatest waste is the effort to deliver what's wrongly designed."

Just as PI (Process Innovation), which abolishes the process without added value, is prerequisite even before establishing ERP, when promoting Industry 4.0, be sure to first, production technology (element technology) and manufacturing technology (management technology) in a physical factory. It is necessary to achieve maximization of work efficiency even in pre-processes such as product development.

In order to achieve this goal, it is important to understand our current status, and data on the status of manufacturing competitiveness of major countries around the world analyzed by the Ministry of Economy, Trade and Industry of Japan will be helpful.

The US has the world's No. 1 manufacturing competitiveness, but Korea has the lowest manufacturing competitiveness, at least among the "major countries" that Japan is conscious of. Because of this variation in each country, the solution companies leading Industry 4.0 are making efforts to provide a common foundation for all companies by creating global standards. However, it is true that the speed is progressing very slowly, but even if it is possible, what changes is there in competitiveness?

Computers are more productive than handwriting, but when everyone is working on computers, the competitive advantage disappears. It is admitted that the solution of Industry 4.0 creates a better environment than it is now, but it is questionable how to secure a competitive advantage by pursuing it if it is a universal solution that can be adopted by all competitors. It will be a necessary condition and not a sufficient condition. International standard means lower limit management. Management is a game with a lower limit but no upper limit.

As we have seen above, Toyotaism is already spreading beyond Toyota to the world, beyond a single company to numerous Lean companies. "It takes a lot of time for new paradigms and knowledge to blossom," said Peter Drucker. It would be nice not to be easily shaken by the slogan of a paradigm change or some kind of revolution when you wake up. As already mentioned, the phenomenon is not the cause, and the trend is not a paradigm.

Chapter 19.

The challenges of a new era found by successful companies in the 21st century

It is said that the owner and the customer have changed. The reason why the phenomenon and the cause has been emphasized continuously is that in many cases, by thinking that the phenomenon is the cause, there are cases of staying in ad-hoc measures or taking wrong actions.

I say this because I want to say that the value or method of Toyotism is an ideal that has already been created, so it is not necessary to understand and follow it. Rather, Toyotism is only the result of finding and contemplating ways with the body and mind to cope with the challenges of the times. In other words, whether it is 'Lean', 'Toyotism' or 'Industrial 4.0', whatever its name, times have changed, and so the task to respond to it has changed, so we want to emphasize that we have to have different actions and philosophy. will be. This is a phenomenon we must face and is a prerequisite. Toyota Motor Co., Ltd. responded to the task earlier than other companies, so it was only the result of what was called "Toyotism". In other words, Toyota Motor Company is only the first to discover the flag even in the dark before dawn at dawn. First of all, because they found the target point, they are only running the shortest path at the present time to reach it.

It should be seen that it is only the beginning that the rules of the new game of our time have been applied. There are still plenty of opportunities. But you should know that the day was bright. Increasingly, companies are aware of the challenges of the new era, and they immediately searched for who responded best. Toyota was the founding company. So what has been benchmarking Toyota over the past decade by so many people and companies has been an effort to find a solution, recognizing that the challenges of their times have changed. Now we also have to get up and run properly.

The new task of corporate survival according to the changing times

Then, what are the tasks of the times in our time? In particular, what are the challenges that companies need to solve? It seems that it can be summarized in a word, "All corporate activities in the 21st century are JIT games." It is to supply goods or services as customers want, what they want, when they want them, and as much as they want. From that point of view, you can see that all the companies on the planet, including Amazon, Dell, Xiaomi, Zara, Tencent, Google, and Alibaba, are eventually heading for the same flag. Although the methods and techniques differ depending on the nature of the business they are targeting.

Fordism's youngest person, who sells what the supplier wants to make or what the supplier wants, when the supplier wants, and as much as the supplier wants, is now enough with Apple. In fact, Apple is a living fossil of Fordism that they mistakenly believe that they can always be in the place of 'Only One'. The era of the German generals, who are mass-producing small items, release them at the price and time they want, and push for the AS policy, has passed. However, it is not extinct yet. The existence of a company like Apple thus confuses people.

The need to build an ecosystem should be recognized as a matter of scope of contribution, not as a monopoly or oligopoly. This is because it goes against the development of the whole society. In that sense, I don't think it is advisable to praise that Apple, which accounts for only 20% of the market share of all mobile phones, accounts for the majority of all profits. The spread of values that make people only look at first place, regardless of who won the first place, causes a conflict with the values of the 21st century. It is only a mistake of hasty generalization that the method of number 1 is correct because it is number one.

From the era of division of labor to the era of collaboration, from an elite solo to an era of teamwork, from control to delegation, from a single-line economy to a circular economy, from mass production of small-sized species to a variety of variable production This shifting production), from intensive production to decentralized production, from the subordination of SMEs to large companies to win-win and cooperative relationships can solve the problem.

Watching Ford in the era of mass production has inspired many companies. Now, we are seeing a number of new companies appearing through Toyota that are recognizing the challenges of a new era and trying to solve them, constantly trying methodologies optimized for their business. It's not too late to go back. Now, it is enough just to get 'Insight' through 'Sight'.

Outro

Dreaming of Resourcism, another name for Toyotism

18 September 2015.

Prince Rashid of Dubai died young at the early age of 33. Born to King Sheikh Mohammed bin Rashid Al Maktoum and Queen Sheikha Alia bint Mohammed bin Butti al Hamed, Prince Rashid was the fittest and eldest son, enough to attract public attention. After graduating from the British Sandhurst Military Academy, he competed in the Doha Asian Games horseback riding national team in Qatar in 2006, winning two gold medals around his neck, raising the honor of the country and the royal family.

He was also an entrepreneur running investment firm United Holdings Group Dubai and racetrack Zabeel Racing International. In addition, it was reported that his assets amounted to 1.9 billion dollars (about 2.24 trillion won) as income from various businesses and inherited assets. In the royal family of Dubai, one of the seven emirates of the United Arab Emirates (UAE), it is common for the eldest son to become crown prince, and he became crown prince early in his childhood.

However, in 2008, in response to the opinion of the royal family that his immediate younger brother, Prince Sheikh Hamdan, was more suitable as a prince, Prince Rashid was disqualified from the crown. And even the second place in the succession to the throne was passed to the third brother, Prince Sheikh Maktoum. The reason he was disqualified as a crown prince is said to have been due to drugs, sex parties, and the murder of a royal torture because he was unable to control his anger. I think this was actually an effect, not a cause, but anyway this unfortunate Middle Eastern prince once said this.

"My grandfather rode a camel. My father also rode a camel. I ride a Mercedes, and my son rides a Land Rover. My son's son will ride a Land Rover, but his son will probably ride a camel again."

I quoted it because it came from the mouth of a prince in the Middle East that comes to mind when it comes to oil.

What is the name of our time? We have lived in the Paleolithic Age, Neolithic Age, Bronze Age, and Iron Age, and we do not know the name of the present where we live.

I agree to call our era, which began with the Industrial Revolution, the "carbon era". This is because the main energy and all by-products that lead to coal, oil and electricity come from carbon. Although the term 'carbon era' is not commonly used, the image of a new era that the world is advocating to solve environmental problems is named the 'low carbon era', and our era may be called the 'carbon era'. Petroleum is the protagonist of this carbon age, and the oil is very short.

Some say that the future of mankind will return to the Stone Age due to energy depletion, while others say that it will open a bright future through the discovery of new alternative energies and new synthetic materials. But it is a gamble that determines the future with this dichotomy. Even now, in deciding something, isn't it important to consider whether it is necessary or not, rather than whether it can be done or not.

The most important criterion for Toyota's value judgment is 'necessity'. Whether you can do it or not, spending money or resources on something you don't need is a 'waste'. Likewise, Toyota's philosophy is to support the attitude that if it is judged 'necessary', whether it is possible or not, all of them will gather wisdom and come up with ideas and must achieve it even after several trials and errors. The mass production era was an era of "overeating" triggered by "deprivation" for millions of years. Even if I don't need it, the fact that I eat more, have a lot, and stack up a lot gave me a feeling of satiety. Addicted to that feeling of satiety, we are faced with the paradox that we have created an era of "infinite competition" despite our progress.

The single-line view of the world and development in the West is struggling with only an attempt to explain today as something better than yesterday. However, humans and wolves have the ability to distribute anywhere in the world because they are animals that know how to collaborate, not compete. Unfortunately, wolves are now endangered. Humans may have tried to erase the traces of collaboration by expelling wolves. However, our "self" still remains. Humans, which are distributed over the widest area in the world and have the most powerful influence, remain. We will need to look back at what made us where we are.

An exhausting war of competition-it's not good to instill the illusion that 'newer is better' in order to make more, sell more, and consume more. It is not desirable to return to the era of riding camels in the end due to the expanded reproduction of "destructive consumption," which is discarded not because things have lost their function but simply because they are old. There are movements around the world to prepare for the era of consuming only what is needed, when necessary, and in the amount necessary. Extensive collaboration is taking place globally to achieve that goal with minimal input, and there is an abundance of people who are willing to present their abilities and resources.

The concept of "access rights that can be used" rather than "ownership," but not "share" or "ownership," is creating a new industry. Thanks to the volunteers' dedication to disseminating knowledge worth disseminating, we have free access to an ecosystem called TED. There is a movement to ensure the right to share rather than own, and access rather than ownership, to all goods beyond cars and homes. As a result, it is realizing the lowest cost.

The image of a society where transaction costs are infinitely low is surprisingly realized not through "competition" but through "collaboration," but it shows a "vision" that we have been familiar with for a very long time. The enthusiasm and active participation of many people in these new businesses and new services makes it even more evident that they are no longer simply consumers as consumers, but prosumers as suppliers and consumers.

Peter Drucker officially declared "the emergence of knowledge workers" and cut off labor relations in the era of mass production. For the past 100 years, whether it is left-wing or right-wing economics, workers and capitalists, workers and employers, the relationship between the two actors has been a dynamic relationship between 'the side that has the means of production' and 'the side that does not have the means of production'. However, by announcing the birth of "a knowledge worker who owns the means of production called knowledge," Peter Drucker announced that the developmental integration of labor-management relations had already been achieved.

It is also necessary to understand that the framework of labor-management relations has fundamentally changed with the end of the mass production era. In the thousands of years before the mass production era, kings, nobles, capitalists, the owners of the means of production, whether they were people, serfs, or workers, could increase their wealth simply by exploiting the labor of those who did not. Industrial capitalists of the past 100 years have also basically achieved such wealth. But not now. Nowadays, no matter how much the capitalist exploits the labor of the workers, they do a lot of work, and no matter how many things they make, there is no way to multiply wealth unless they are sold. This is the fundamental cause of the tensions that arise in today's industrial relations.

If both labor and management are not sold, there is no way

to increase wealth. Nevertheless, as in the past, the demand for a higher salary since labor was put in, or the demand to work harder because the business is unstable is only raising tension without a solution. Labor and management must work together to achieve the corporate purpose that the company declared to contribute to society. By doing so, it must shift to a way that the customer approves it and shares the profits that the customer is willing to pay for its value.

The role of management can be said to be decision-making on material resources and decision-making on human resources. Management is also an activity that produces maximum output with minimum input. So management is about doing extraordinary things with ordinary people. However, the role of such management is shifting from one CEO to each member and each person. That is, leadership is no longer a matter of status. In addition, the word to become a knowledge worker is a declaration that one person and one person who possesses "knowledge and labor as means of production" are the chief executives. All managers should try to get the maximum output with the minimum input. However, the output is not a "goal" expressed in numbers such as sales or profit. It refers to the achievement of the business objective of providing goods and services to customers 'what they need, when they need it, and in the amount they need'. When the purpose of the business is achieved, profits follow. It doesn't make sense to offer a product or service to be sold and that it is not profitable.

Also, we must remember that the creation of ideal information has a higher profit than the transcription of ideal information. It should be noted that the added value is determined by the quality, which is the result of transcription of ideal information. It must be carefully observed that the comparative advantage of material resources is gradually disappearing due to the development of production technology and manufacturing technology.

It is now a world that everyone acknowledges that it is impossible to maintain competitiveness in the market forever by increasing the amount of input of material resources. It has become a world in which the comparative advantage is cleared by human resources that create creative ideal information and come up with ideas to solve problems that are revealed in transcription. Since there is the same movement in human resources, 'Work Smart' becomes important.

Low labor productivity (output) despite long working hours (input) is the strongest sign that the company's management is overall failing. Nevertheless, many executives think that they will succeed if they 'work harder enough and make more enough' because companies that are successful with more inputs have not yet gone extinct. In doing so, Toyota also fell in 1950. This is why management should be careful about "wasting" human resources.

Amid increasing signs of dependence on physical resources and physical constraints, the dependence on human resources in business activities is bound to increase. The subject of creating and transcribing ideal information must be humans. Nevertheless, the development of ICT and intelligent robots will make many jobs disappear and many industries disappear. Many jobs will disappear. As it has been, new jobs will also be created with the advancement of the industry. No, rather, a new way of doing things will be born.

The new 'work' and 'method' of work will be carried out through collaboration, not division of labor. The paradigm for the new 'work' and 'the way of work' to be unfolded in the 21st century is constructed by the fundamental question of 'necessary', not whether it is possible or not. Customers are already starting to ask. Do you really need this? Do you need to own this? Going back to that question, the effort to achieve that goal while consuming our resources to a minimum is emerging as a huge business. Uberna Airbnb is procuring all of its physical and human resources from the cars and homes that the participants have and their labor. In the end, we are exploring a new growth mechanism driven only by the current "material resources" and "human resources".

Beyond capitalism, which is a function of the amount of input and output of resources, we see the "Resourcism" created by the world's people. After grasping only the core of what they need, they look around and ask. Who can do this? Who has this? Such consensus people are creating what they need, when and as much as they need with the least amount of resources.

As a result, the question of whether a "company" is absolutely necessary is growing. This is probably the reason why co-operatives and numerous non-profit organizations are created. Those who say that the purpose of a company is 'pursuing profits' should know that the atmosphere around them is changing. There are no customers who spend it for the "profit" of a company.

People who sympathize with the ideology and values of the company, the validity of the ideal information to be realized by the product and service, and the dedication to the company. And, like Fair Trade, people who look at the legitimacy of the transcription process and resonate with such companies. If there is no such good company, those who start such companies themselves. As such people create a leading trend, Resourceism is emerging.

The sharing economy is a concept proposed by Harvard

University professor Lawrence Lessig as an alternative to overcome this recession when the global economy faces a crisis after the 2008 financial crisis. According to Professor Lawrence, the sharing economy refers to the whole activity in which individuals or companies share their assets or services, which increases the availability of assets and reduces the burden of ownership, which promotes economic growth and realizes sustainability. That is his argument.

Starting with Airbnb, a platform for sharing accommodation, in 2008, sharing services in various fields began to penetrate into everyday life, and in 2019, more than 7 out of 10 Americans answered that they have provided or experienced sharing services. It has become a part of everyday life. Airbnb, which implements the world's largest lodging business without owning a single property such as a hotel, or Uber, has grown the vehicle industry to the world's largest without owning a single car. They were constantly being talked about as innovative success stories of companies, and in tandem with the tendency of the present generation to worry about sustainability, they began to be recognized as about the next stage of the current industry. It is in this context that I am talking of Resourcism.

However, due to the corona, there was a concern that everything would be lost.

In fact, humanity has overcome the threat of bacteria and viruses without giving in, and the process has also become a part of history. However, the daily routine that was taken for granted to us was no longer taken for granted, and we became suspicious of everything we thought was safe. When our lives have changed, it means that many things related to life are bound to change as well. In particular, in many industries where human-to-person contact is essential, fundamental change is required due to COVID19. As we enter the era of maximizing fear related to contact, one of the industries that is hit hardest is Share Business, that is, the sharing economy industry.

In recent years, companies based in the sharing economy have seen remarkable growth worldwide. Airbnb, which made the hotel industry tense, Uber, which threatened the life and death of the taxi industry, and WeWork, which showed a new paradigm of office space. It has emerged as the most preferred company for young talent, and the company's asset value has grown to over tens of billions of dollars. Of course, a number of companies advocating or benchmarking the second Airbnb, Uber, and WeWork have sprung up.

However, as a highly contagious virus, which no one

expected, spreads in the world, the sharing economy faced a limit in a completely different aspect. As it becomes impossible to travel, it is expected that Airbnb's loss in the first half of this year will exceed 1 trillion won. In China, more than 90% of the number of users has decreased, and in Korea and Italy, the number of users has decreased by 50%. It may be said that everything is timing, but COVID19 will be particularly harsh for Airbnb, which is about to go public this year.

Uber is also difficult. Even before the COVID19 crisis, it was difficult enough to cut more than 1,200 people last year due to various problems such as friction with the existing industry, but the situation became even more disastrous with the spread of COVID 19. According to CEO Dara Kosroshahi, in Seattle, the US, Uber usage has decreased by more than 70% since the coronavirus outbreak. As people are reluctant to go out, the number of passengers has declined, resulting in a decline in driver income, leading to deterioration in the company's management.

WeWork, a representative of the shared office company, quickly became unclear about the pinkish future after the failure to go public last year. At a time in the midst of a crisis situation, the spread of Corona 19 made WeWork face another ordeal. Sharing office space with others is starting to turn into fear rather than new. From the breakup with investors and the decline of users, this year is expected to be a year at the crossroads of life and death for WeWork in many ways.

As mentioned earlier, the sharing economy simply means conducting economic activities through the act of sharing assets through "rental" rather than "owning". Before the virus became so prevalent, sharing was a great concept for this era. However, at this point when distancing becomes a virtue, sharing something with someone you don't know appears as a negative image. Softbank CEO Masayoshi Son, who is called "Midas's Hand," was Uber and WeWork, sharing economy companies that boldly invested in thinking that it was the future of the industry, but he did not even anticipate the bad news of COVID19. After WeWork's failed IPO, Sohn soothed investors, saying that spring will come after a brutal winter. If COVID19 is over and social distancing is over, will the spring of mind come, where you can casually contact others?

The Korean CCO Club, a group of former and current large corporations in charge of public relations, surveyed readers of "Finance Insights," a magazine published by the Federation of Korean Industries, about "what are the words of entrepreneurs who feel the entrepreneurial spirit best". As a result of the investigation, it is said that the late Chairman Ju-young Chung's "Hey, have you tried it?" was selected as number one.

We must pay the price of the mass production era pursued for 230 years in the Anglo-American region, 100 years in Japan, and decades in Korea and China. Climate change and epidemic outbreaks are signals the planet sends to us. The methods so far are showing that they are no longer sustainable. They blindly conquered and exploited resources, nature and the environment. Earth is showing that it shouldn't be any more.

In retrospect, whenever we realized something, we believed we could do it, and we did it well.

Use only what you really need, when you need it, and as much as you need it.

So, isn't this the question of the age in which we will live?

"Hey, do you really need that?"

References

PDCA starting with C, Japan Efficiency Association Management Center , 2013

40 years after reaching S-level, Toshiaki Takahashi, 2007

Visible management, Hiroshi Ishibashi, 2005

Visibility practice, Hideaki Masaki, 2008

All Visible or Realizable Workbook, Honmichi Junichi, 2009

Google vs Toyota, Ryosuke Izumida, 2014

Monozukuri Management Innovation, Japan Efficiency Association, 2001

Toyota Manufacturing System, Toyota Manufacturing System Study Group, 2008

Supply Chain Management Revolution, Fukushima Bimei, 1998

Introduction to Production Management, Takahiro Fujimoto, 2001

Post-Toyota, Hideharu Kaneda, 1993

Hands-on IT Toyota Manufacturing, Fujitsu Prime Software Technology, 2005

Why would anyone think in A3, Sumie Ishii, 2015?

Introduction to Toyota Production System, Masamitsu Ishii, 2005

Why Japan's Automotive Industry Is Strong, Takahiro Fujimoto, 2007

Manufacturing High Level Objective Management Act, Kenichi Omi, 2006

Production philosophy beyond manufacturing, Takahiro Fujimoto, 2007

product development capabilities, Takahiro Fujimoto, 2009

In the era of Talent, Takao Sakai, 2015

How strong is Toyota, Nikkei Business, 2002

Toyota Style Success Note, Yoshito Wakamatsu, 2004

Toyota New Industrial Revolution, Aiichiro Mizushima, 2005

Toyota Production Counterattack, Naohisa Suzumura, 2015

Toyota Production System Cross-industry Development Practice, Mitsumasa Kumazawa, 2015

Toyota Production System Book, Toyota Production System Study Group, 2004

Toyota System and International Strategy, Kiichi Kagiyama, 2003

Toyota Prevention Method, Tatsuhiko Yoshimura, 2002

Toyota Job Basics, OJT Solutions, 2015

Toyota Stupid Human Resource Development, Inoue Hisao, 2007

Techniques for putting together one piece of paper learned at Toyota, Asada Kururu, 2015

Toyota Way's Most Powerful Management Technique, Kazuaki Kajiwara, 2002

Toyota CSR Strategy, Ken Sakuma, 2006

Toyota common sense, Hiroki Hoshikawa, 2002

Toyota's brain challenged the strongest TQM, Araga, 2002

Toyota Product Development, Eiji Adachi, 2014

Toyota Motor Corporation Chief Investigator System,

Shigeru Shiozawa, 1987

History of Toyota Motor Corporation, Koichiro Takahashi, 2014

Kiichiro Toyota, Masatsugu Kimoto, Yuya Kagemaru, 1994

Toyota Production System, Yasuhiro Koda, 2006

Toyota Information System Supporting Toyotaism, Masaaki Toda, 2006

www.ingramcontent.com/pod-product-compliance
Lightning Source LLC
Chambersburg PA
CBHW020634220526
45464CB00001B/142